1:

The Ferret and Ferreting Handbook

The Ferret and Ferreting Handbook

James McKay

The Crowood Press

First published in 1989 by
The Crowood Press Ltd
Ramsbury, Marlborough
Wiltshire SN8 2HR

This impression 2001

British Library Cataloguing-in-Publication Data

A catalogue record for this book is available from the British Library

ISBN 1-85223-772-4

Acknowledgements
Photographs by James McKay
Line-drawings by Jane Frith

Typeset by Alacrity Phototypesetters, Banwell Castle,
Weston-super-Mare, Avon.
Printed in Great Britain by Redwood Books, Trowbridge, Wiltshire

Dedication

To Jane, for having faith.

Contents

Introduction

Love them or hate them, ferrets hold a fascination for most people, be they very young or somewhat older. For me, the fascination started when I was 8 years old but, as my parents would not allow me to keep them, I had to wait until I had a place of my own before owning any ferrets. That was almost twenty years ago and since then there has never been a time when I did not possess at least a pair of these marvellous creatures.

During my time with ferrets, I have read books, listened to sage advice from many an 'old timer' and, most importantly, gained the experience of keeping and working ferrets of many different sizes and temperaments. I have sifted through all the information that has come my way concerning these fascinating animals and much of it could best be described as misinformation, some as old wives' tales and some as pure claptrap! In this book, I am attempting to put the story straight, to dispose of the many myths and to give the ferret some of the good publicity that she so richly deserves. Not everyone will agree with what I have to say. All that I can say is that all of the methods described in this book have served me – and my ferrets – well for almost twenty years. Nothing contained in this volume is written from mere hearsay or has been passed on from a third party; it is all taken from my own practical experiences. If it has worked for me, then it will probably work for you.

Ferrets have had a lot of bad publicity in the past, and have been the butt of many jokes and unkind words. Anyone who has actually spent time with ferrets, and especially those who have worked them, will tell you that they are some of the most intelligent, clean, playful and brave creatures that live on this earth. Too long have they been the subject of comedians' humour. Authors of fiction, who describe ferrets and their relatives as sly, evil creatures, have obviously never met a real ferret or weasel, or they would know just how inaccurate that description is. If, by writing this book, I have persuaded a few more people to think better of the ferret, then my efforts have not been wasted.

In this book, I have tried to give all the advice that I would have liked when I first began keeping ferrets in the early 1970s. This information will obviously be of use to the tyro, but I hope that it will also be useful and informative to those who have kept ferrets for some time. None of us know enough about ferrets. We can all learn more.

I would like to express my gratitude to the many people who have helped and encouraged me in the production of this book, including Tom Alexander, who not only appears in many of the photographs but also read through my original manuscripts and advised me on their content and readability; Inspector John Thornley, who gave his advice on the section dealing with the law; Noel Walker, BVSc., MRCVS, who gave his advice on the section dealing with ferret first aid and ailments; to John Harradine, who helped with the photography; and to Norah Frith, who very kindly allowed me to publish details of some of the rabbit recipes that have been in her family for many years.

James McKay

9

1
Origins

'I believe that our domestic animals were originally chosen by uncivilised men because they were useful.'

Charles Darwin

The domesticated ferret, commonly seen as a working animal involved in the control of such pests as the rabbit and the rat, is descended from the wild European polecat. Indeed, not only does the dark type of ferret (often referred to as a 'poley', a 'polecat-ferret' or even simply – though misleadingly – as a 'polecat') share the looks of her wild cousin, she also shares its Latin, or scientific name, *Mustella putorius*. (The name means, quite literally, 'smelly weasel'!) It is common for the ferret (of whatever colour) to be referred to as *Mustella putorius furo*, '*furo*' meaning thief, possibly due to the fact that the ferret is, and always has been, linked with poachers – thieves by another name.

The ferret belongs to the weasel tribe, or *mustelidae*, and is thus related to such animals as the otter, badger and the skunk. She is also a carnivore, and thus related to cats (including lions and tigers), dogs (including wolves and foxes) and civets (meercats and mongooses).

Scientific Classification of the Ferret

Order *Carnivora* (7 families; 93 genera; 231 species)
This order embraces cats (including lions and tigers), dogs (including foxes, jackals and wolves), bears (including polar and grizzly), racoons (including coatis and giant pandas), weasels (including stoats and polecats), civets (including meercats and mongooses) and hyenas.

Family *Mustelidae* (26 genera; 67 species)
The *mustelidae* are to be found all over the world, in every continent except Australia and Antarctica. Their habitat ranges from arctic tundra to tropical rainforest, on land, in trees, in rivers and in the ocean. Animals in this tribe range in size from the diminutive least weasel (*Mustella nivalis rixosa*), which measures 15cm (6in) head to tail with a tail length of 3 – 4cm (1½in) and weighs as little as 30g (1oz), to the massive bulk of the grison (*Galictis vittata*), a mammal from Central and South America, which resembles a wolverine and can attain sizes of up to 120cm (48in) head to tail with a tail of up to 65cm (26in) and weighs in at up to 30kg (66lb)!

Sub-Family *Mustelinae* (10 genera; 33 species)
These include the grisons, martens, mink, polecats and weasels.

Members of the Sub-Family Mustelinae

M. africana   the tropical weasel
M. altaica   the mountain weasel
M. erminea   the common stoat (ermine)
M. eversmanni   the Steppe polecat
M. felipei   the Columbian weasel
M. frenata   the long tailed weasel
M. kathiah   the yellow bellied weasel
M. lutreola   the European mink
M. lutreolina   the Indonesian mountain weasel
M. nigripes   the black footed ferret*
M. nivalis   the European common weasel
M. nivalis rixosa   the least weasel

The Polecat.

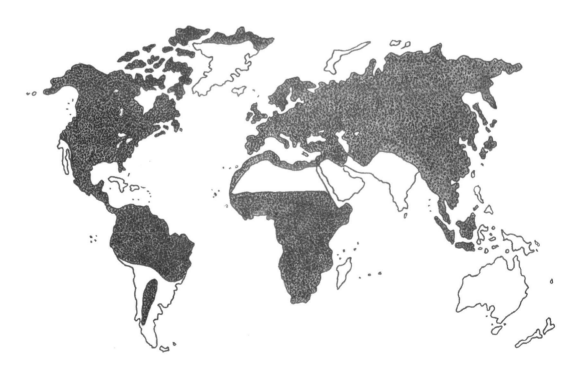

World distribution of weasels and polecats.

M. nudipes   the Malaysian weasel
M. putorius   the European polecat
M. putorius furo   the domesticated ferret
M. sibirica   the Siberian weasel
M. strigidorsa   the back striped weasel
M. vison   the American mink
Vormela peregusna   the marbled polecat
Martes americana   the American marten
M. flavigula   the yellow throated marten
M. foina   the beech marten
M. martes   the pine marten
M. melampus   the Japanese marten
M. pennanti   the fisher
M. zibellina   the sable
Eira barbata   the tayra
Galictis cuja   the little grison
G. vittata   the greater grison
Lyncodon patagonicus   the Patagonian weasel
Ictonyx striatus   the Zorilla, or striped polecat
Poecilictis libyca   the Saharan striped weasel
Poecilogale albinucha   the white naped weasel
Gulo   the wolverine

* The black footed ferret, at one time thought to be extinct, is extremely rare, due to both human interference and disease. After being 'rediscovered', the black footed ferret is now the subject of captive breeding projects and various research programmes. It is the only member of the weasel tribe to be listed as 'endangered' by the International Union for the Conservation of Nature (IUCN).

The Ferret's Introduction

It is not known for certain when the first ferret, or more likely semi-tame polecat, was first introduced into Britain for sporting purposes, i.e. to help its owner catch rabbits for food. Almost every book and other authority disagrees with the next one. One thing does, however, seem obvious to me – the introduction of this wonderful, tame (i.e. not afraid of humans) predator must have been linked with the introduction of that other foreign invader – the rabbit.

It is believed by some authorities that the rabbit was introduced to Britain by the Romans, to supplement their rations and to ensure that, wherever Rome's legions marched, there would be food available. The Romans were well known for their liking of the meat of small mammals and tended to take them wherever they travelled. They even brought the Edible Dormouse (*Glis glis*) to England. The animals were kept in earthenware jars until they were fat enough to provide more than a couple of mouthfuls of meat and then killed and cooked with fruit and nuts before being served.

Other authorities believe that it was the Normans who introduced the rabbit, again as a source of food. We will probably never know for sure, but it seems likely that whoever was responsible for the introduction of the rabbit was also responsible for the first use of the domesticated polecat, or ferret, in Britain. It is, however, certain that the ferret has been around for a very long time (at least 1,500 years) in other parts of the world, where she has been used to help her owners to catch their food.

The first historical mention of a ferret is said to be that of Aristophanes (*circa* 450BC) in the comedy *The Acharnians*. Another ancient mention was by Aristotle (*circa* 320BC) in his *Historia Animalium*. However, both references are rather controversial, since scholars cannot agree on the correct translation from the Greek. The first truly accepted reference to the ferret was by Strabo (*circa* 63BC) in his *Geographica*. He writes of a Libyan animal which was specifically bred and introduced to rabbit burrows to either bolt the rabbits or hang on to them while the animal, complete with captured rabbit, was dragged out on the end of its lead. This animal was always used muzzled, and is said to have held its quarry in its claws! That this is evidence of a ferret being worked is substantiated by the fact that a tribe in Morocco, the Ruafa, still employ such methods, using a ferret.

Pliny mentions both the ferret and the rabbit, in *circa* 23AD in his *Natural History* and, in 600AD, Isadore of Seville, wrote of the ferret's use in rabbit hunting (*Patrologie*). The rabbit, whose history is inexorably linked with that of the ferret, was originally indigenous to Spain and North Africa and, by the end of the first century AD, was firmly ensconced in Southern France.

By the Middle Ages, the ferret was widely used for hunting the rabbit and, in his *Livre de Chasse* (*circa* 1387), Gaston, Comte de Foix, shows drawings of ferreting taking place, complete with a muzzled ferret and several purse nets. It is also said that the infamous Genghis Khan used ferrets in 1221, at Termez, a place on the banks of the River Oxus, about 160 miles south of Samarkand (Afghanistan).

The first concrete evidence of ferrets and their use against rabbits, in Britain, is to be found in a court roll of 1223. There are also references to a ferreter being attached to the Royal Court in 1281. At that time, rabbits, and thus ferrets, were very important to the church and its establishments, as can be seen by the many references to ferrets belonging to quite high ranking churchmen of the time. In 1390, a law was passed limiting the ownership of ferrets to those with a minimum salary of forty shillings per annum, possibly in an attempt to keep them out of the hands of would-be poachers. Rabbits were at this time very important to the local economy.

Characteristics

Most weasels and polecats weigh 2kg (4lb) or less, with large differences in size between the sexes (the males are larger than the females). Weasels and polecats all move with a characteristic gait – almost wave-like. All are terrestrial hunters of great ability, able to take prey many times larger than themselves. For example the weasel can (and does) take rabbits which are several times bigger and heavier than they are themselves. Polecats and weasels are almost entirely carnivorous and their teeth are ideally suited to the job of first killing and then cutting up their prey. As with most carnivorous mammals, they tend to kill their prey with a bite on the back of the animal's neck.

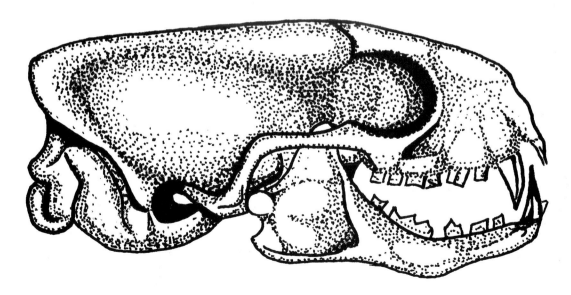

The polecat skull. Note the teeth – ideally suited to killing and cutting up their prey.

Many members of the *mustelidae* are renowned for the quality of their fur, a fact that has sometimes led to the over hunting of certain species and also to their being bred in captivity in order to ensure a ready supply of skins for such things as fur coats. The mink is probably the most obvious example.

All species have anal glands. These glands produce a thick, oily and extremely strong smelling secretion, referred to as 'musk'. This is used by the animals to mark their territories and also as a deterrent against would-be predators. Even domesticated ferrets can discharge some of this fluid if they are provoked enough, or fear for their lives. In this, the ferret certainly deserves its Latin name; trying to remove the smell from clothes is a lost cause!

The only time that I have experienced this, was when I had to capture an escaped hob ferret (owner unknown) which had been living wild in some allotment gardens in Yorkshire. He had obviously got used to being his own boss and was rather annoyed at being enticed into a trap from which he could not escape. He showed his annoyance in no uncertain way when I removed him from the trap to put him into a cage. In the end, I had to throw my clothes away, as no-one would come within ten metres of me! Alf, as I called him, soon settled down, however, and became one of the nicest ferrets that I have had the privilege to meet. He was used as a stud, producing some of the best working (and easily handled) ferrets that I have ever come across. I still have one of his daughters, Izzy, who is capable of a good day's hunting, despite her age (ten years at the time of writing).

It is quite normal for a little musk to be passed out with the animal's faeces, marking territory. Some pet owners do not like the idea of their ferrets ever having a chance of discharging this obnoxious smelling fluid however, and have their veterinary surgeon remove the anal gland. This is a very controversial subject, and many vets will refuse to carry out the operation on ethical grounds. However, some vets will remove the gland and I have met several 'de-glanded' ferrets, none of whom seem to have suffered any harm from the operation. I would not recommend owners to have their pets operated on in this manner, however, and I would suggest that the matter is given much thought (in consultation with a qualified vet) before any decision is made.

The reproductive habits and characteristics of *mustelids* deserve some mention here. For most of the time in the wild, the sexes keep themselves to themselves and, when they do meet, they are often extremely hostile towards one another. It is only when the female is in oestrus (on heat) that a truce is called. Then the male takes hold of the female by the scruff of the neck, often almost brutally, and proceeds to drag her around until he finds a suitable 'honeymoon site', where he then mounts her.

Copulation is prolonged and repeated (it can last for over two hours) and this is facilitated by the baculum of the male (a bone in the penis). The mating often seems to be almost a fight between the male and female. This is probably nature's way of ensuring that only the strongest pass on their characteristics to the next generation since, if the male cannot 'overpower' the female, he will not be able to mate with her.

In some *mustelids*, delayed implantation occurs. This is where the fertilised egg simply floats around in the uterus until being implanted in the uterus wall at a later date. This date can be anything from a few days to almost one year! (This is not the case with the ferret).

Some Facts About the Ferret

Average weight (adult) – between 400g and 2kg (14oz and 4lb)

Average size (adult) – between 35 and 60cm (13 and 23in)

Average lifespan (in captivity) – between 8 and 12 years

Age at puberty – 250 days (approx)

Age at sexual maturity – 8 to 12 months

Normal breeding season (Britain) – early March to late September

Duration of oestrus – ceases when mated; if unmated, will continue to end of 'season', often causing medical problems

Gestation (pregnancy) – 40 to 44 days

Number of young (in one litter) – 1 to 14 (average 6 to 8) (jills (females) can have up to two litters per year)

Weight at birth – 10g (½oz)

State at birth – blind, deaf, naked and entirely dependent upon the mother

Ears/eyes open – 22 to 36 days

Fur – in dark coloured kits, starts to appear within 5 to 7 days. Good covering by 4 weeks

Movement – kits as young as 2 to 3 weeks will manage to crawl out of the nest (to be dragged back by the mother)

Weaning – 7 to 9 weeks

Weight at weaning – between 300 and 450g (10 and 15oz)

Age attain adult weight – 4 to 5 months

Minimum selling/buying age – 12 weeks

The Attractions of Ferrets

Ferrets are intelligent and clean; even though they do have a characteristic smell they have excellent habits, always using the same area for defecating and urinating. They keep their fur meticulously clean and spend long hours grooming themselves. They are also entertaining to watch as they go through their everyday antics. Watching a ferret trying to break an egg will keep anyone enthralled for hours; I often wonder, at the risk of sounding anthropomorphic, if the ferret really is trying to break the egg, or simply playing with it. The ferret always seems to be enjoying the act so, and almost looks rather sad when, at last and inevitably, the sticky fluid emerges from a crack in the egg's shell.

Ferrets are suitable to be kept for sport (the hunting of rabbits and/or rats), or as pets. In many states in the USA, it is an offence to use ferrets for hunting, but they are very common

All mustelids *have a natural curiosity.*

pets in that country. Ferrets are big enough (and tough enough) to be handled by young children. If the children get a little too rough, as children are inclined to, the ferret will give a warning nip! This need not be alarming or dangerous if the ferret is used to regular handling.

A few years ago, I spent the summer months travelling around the country to various country fairs, putting on displays with my ferrets and some equipment for the British Field Sports Society. At these events, it was common for the public to ask about the ferrets' reputed 'viciousness'. Then, (and on many other occasions), several ferrets were lifted from their cages and offered to members of the crowd which always gathered around such displays. As all of my ferrets are regularly handled from a very early age (some even from birth), I had no worries. On one such occasion I placed Izzy, my favourite jill, on the top of the display while I gave an impromptu talk on the merits of the ferret (I never need much of an excuse for this!) While I was talking, a young girl began blowing in Izzy's face and generally tormenting her. Izzy bristled and began making warning noises. I saw what was happening and interrupted my talk to ask the girl not to torment the ferrets. A few minutes later, Izzy was again warning the girl and I again warned her myself, as did the girl's mother. To no avail; the girl continued her teasing and I was just about to tell her again when Izzy decided that she had had enough. She uttered a loud 'chatter', and ran across the top of the display and wormed her way into my coat pocket – her favourite travelling area and one where she knew that she would not be bothered by ill-mannered humans! Izzy, even during extreme provocation, had been the perfect lady that I always knew she was!

The ferret has much to offer and is the ideal working companion – or pet – for those people who are willing to accept the responsibility and give the time, regular handling and conversation that is needed.

2

Selection of Stock

'A fool must now and then be right by chance.'
William Cowper

Ferrets can live for over ten years if they are well looked after. At the time of writing, I have a jill who is ten years old and still likes to go hunting. It should be obvious, therefore, that one's original stock needs to be chosen with the greatest of care, if they are to serve the purpose for which they are obtained. Breeding is, almost definitely, something that all ferret owners will aspire to and, as bad stock can only breed bad stock, great care must be exercised at the beginning of the venture.

I assume that if you are taking the time and trouble to read this book, you are already one of the more enlightened members of the human race, one who recognises and admires the qualities that ferrets and their relatives possess! You will realise that the term 'ferret', when applied to a shifty human, is a gross misrepresentation of the facts. Well-handled and cared for ferrets are not sly, devious or untrustworthy; neither do they bite without good reason. For several years, I travelled around the country show circuit with my ferrets. During this time, literally thousands of people have handled them – some none too gently – and not one finger has ever been nipped, let alone bitten. There is no such thing as a nasty ferret, only misguided and thought-less owners.

Ask around and you will receive conflicting views on what makes a 'good ferret'. Some will tell you that all albinos (white with pink eyes) are susceptible to illness and are gener-ally weak. Others will say that 'poleys' (natural coloured) are too wild and will never be completely tame. You will hear the often quoted (but untrue) view that only white ferrets should be worked, as their dark coloured relations cannot be so easily spotted when out working in dense cover. As it is necessary for all of one's senses to be finely tuned and alert to all that is happening during any hunting trip, failure to see a ferret exit from a burrow should not be blamed on the ferret's colour, rather on the handler, who was clearly not doing his job efficiently.

Size is another contentious issue; some favour giant ferrets while others go for tiny 'greyhound' types. There are pros and cons to every school of thought and, if you are to remain happy with your original choice – and their future progeny – it is best that all schools of thought are examined thoroughly.

Sex

The hob (male), is usually considerably larger (up to thirty per cent larger) than the jill (female) and is, therefore, less often worked. This is not to say that they cannot be worked, and I have used many hobs successfully over the years. I feel that it may well be due to the fact that the male does not produce young and, as many ferreters wish to see fresh stock every year, few bother to keep hobs. When the time comes for their jills to be mated, the owners simply borrow a hob from a friend. While this can be advantageous, it can also be dangerous in that, without one's own hob, it is almost impossible to develop a 'line' (as described in Chapter 5), the result being that litters vary in size, number of young, character and many other features. If you do decide to rely upon other owners' hobs, ensure that you check the quality and nature of the hob before you decide to use it; this will help ensure that you breed the type of ferret that you really want.

Initially, I would recommend that two jills are kept, as ferrets like company of their own kind and two hobs, unless kept together from a very early age, may fight, especially during the breeding season. A hob and a jill kept together will inevitably produce young, bringing with them the problems of space, food and handling. A couple of years' experience are needed before breeding should be embarked on. (*See* Chapter 5.)

If you are not intending to use one of the many electronic ferret detectors that are on the market, a 'liner' is essential. This is a large hob who is kept on his own and, in the event of a lay-up, is sent into the burrow attached to a long line (hence the name) to find the dead rabbit, move the errant free-working ferret and then curl up next to the rabbit's body. You then dig along the line (which is marked every metre (yard) or so) until you find the liner and rabbit – easier said than done! The liner must, of course, be big and strong enough to pull the line through all the tunnels and then frighten away the free-working ferret. (*See* Chapter 7 for more details.)

With the advent of good quality, efficient and relatively cheap electronic ferret detectors, liners have almost become a thing of the past, with more and more people turning to new technology, and ignoring the old ways. While this is, in itself, not a bad thing, it should always be remembered that even high technology equipment can break down. At such times, it is reassuring to know that you have more than one string to your bow. The possession of, and experience with, a good liner will often prove to be of incalculable benefit to those who regularly work their ferrets. I would always advise any newcomer to the sport to use a liner for at least two seasons of regular work and then to try an electronic detector. I must admit that since I first tried one of these marvellous inventions, I have never worked my ferrets without one. (Ferret detectors are discussed fully in Chapter 8.)

Albino or Polecat?

The colour of your ferrets will matter only to you. There are no obvious differences in the character of the colours, nor in their working

An albino ferret.

Choice of colour will not influence working abilities.

ability. Some ferreters insist on only albinos since, so they say, the whitish fur will always show up well in the undergrowth; for exactly the same reason, others will say that dark colours are best, as most ferreting takes place in the winter months when there is a strong possibility of snow on the ground. Neither are wholly correct. If you are ferreting and are not so alert that you will see or hear a ferret leaving a burrow, then you should not be working your ferrets, although if working in areas of particularly dense cover (such as brambles) it is possible to miss the emergence of a ferret, particularly a dark coloured animal. If you like light colours, keep those; if you prefer dark ones, then they are the ones for you. Personally, I have kept albinos, polecats and almost every colour in between. They have all worked as well as I have allowed them to and the only one to make mistakes has been me.

I like to see some variety in my stock and, providing that the ferret is a good worker, colour is completely immaterial to me. It is possible to breed ferrets of a particular colour, e.g. all polecats, all white, some of each and

perhaps some colours which are neither one nor the other. To do this, one needs to have a working knowledge of simple Mendelian genetics and to know the breeding and parentage (for at least three generations) of all of one's ferrets. Even with all of this knowledge, the actual results may never be exactly as those worked out on paper! (Details of the genetic aspects of selective colour breeding are to be found in Chapter 5.)

Size

Ferrets come in a wide variety of shapes and sizes, all with their own adherents and champions. The arguments put forward to support each are numerous; large ferrets have more stamina (they also have more weight to carry), small ferrets are faster (but have less stamina), large ferrets are easier to see and can drag rabbits out of stops (dead ends), small ferrets can actually climb over such rabbits and thus flush them out of the stop. I have tried most types and am a great believer in the smaller ferrets. They should not be so small that they tire within five minutes of being put into a hole, but neither should they be so large that they cannot easily pass through the mesh of an average purse net (without disturbing the net).

Smaller ferrets seem to be able to climb over the backs of rabbits which have set themselves into a stop, with their nose against the wall and back feet kicking out viciously. This ability seems to result in fewer lay-ups (i.e. killed rabbits which are eaten by the ferret, who then decides to take forty winks). Larger ferrets will simply scratch and eat away at the back of the rabbit, until the animal is dead. This almost always results in lost meat and digging – not what the sport is all about.

A legend has grown up around a very small strain of ferrets, known as 'greyhound ferrets'. These ferrets are (or perhaps were) very tiny – never more than about fifteen to twenty centimetres (six to eight inches) long – and extremely quick moving. They were said to be able to flush any rabbit out of a stop and also to take on, out manoeuvre and then kill any rat – no matter what size – that they encountered. I have met many people who are trying to breed such animals; I have also met some people who claim to own such animals. However, I have never actually met any of these ferrets. I am not saying that they have not existed in the past, or that they do not exist today, just that I have never actually encountered one of them. Every sport and hobby has its own legends and tales of outstanding characters and events, but I do wonder if these ferrets are a figment of imagination, rather like the massive fish that always eludes capture by the angler and, somehow, always seems to get bigger with every telling of the story.

Age

Never buy older ferrets. If a ferret is good at her job, no amount of money will persuade the owner to part with her. There always has to be a good reason for the animal being offered for sale – usually something to do with her bad habits! Likewise, it is as well to avoid purchasing stock at the country fairs, as many of these are from questionable backgrounds and you will never have the opportunity to vet the parents and the conditions that the ferrets have been kept in.

Choose ferrets of between four and six months. At this age they will show their adult characteristics, while still being young enough to be moulded to your own ideas. Never buy a ferret of less than twelve weeks of age, as these should still be with their mothers, being fed and cared for by them. A ferret kit (a baby ferret) is not fully weaned until at least twelve weeks of age. I have seen ferrets as young as four weeks offered for sale by unscrupulous and uncaring owners. Such animals usually come from very poor living conditions and have been bred with only one purpose in mind – financial profit. It is illegal – not to mention immoral – to sell any animal that is not completely weaned and, if you witness such a sale, or attempted sale, (and this, unfortunately, is usually at one of the many country shows held all over Britain throughout the summer), report it immediately to the event organisers and, if at all possible, to the local RSPCA official. The sooner such dealings are stamped out, the better – for ferrets and responsible ferret owners.

It will be obvious from these guidelines that the best time of year to look for new stock is between June and November, when there is a good selection of young ferrets offered for sale. Do not rush into any purchase, especially of an animal, as you will be taking on the responsibility of ensuring that it is properly fed, housed, receives appropriate medical treatment and, generally, has a good and happy life. Such responsibilities take time, effort and money.

Purchasing Stock

It is possible to buy ferrets for less than £1 from individuals at country fairs, or even from the columns of the local newspaper; this is not

Ferrets are often sold at country fairs, but this is not the best way to ensure that good, healthy stock are obtained.

Mother and kits should be seen together.

recommended. Decide what colour, size, sex and quantity you require and then approach an established breeder. If you do not know of any, contact your local club (the name and address of the secretary can be obtained from the secretary of the National Ferret Welfare Society, *see* Appendix 1), who will be able to help. It may also be possible for the Ferret Welfare Society to arrange for an experienced ferreter to accompany you on your tour of inspection, giving you the benefit of their experience.

Arrange to see the ferrets, in their cage and with their parent(s), in order that you can see for yourself the conditions in which they have been kept. If you are intending to purchase stock on this visit, do not forget to take a good carrying box (filled with a good quantity of hay) with you. Do not expect the breeder to give you the hard sell; he will be scrutinising you, since no true ferreter will sell his stock to just anyone!

Look at the cage – is it large enough? Is it clean? Are there any pieces of uneaten, mouldy food? Look at and handle the parent(s) of the litter. Are they tame and at ease with you? Are they in good condition? (Bear in mind that a nursing mother will not be as plump and fit as she would be at other times.) Are they clean? (Pay particular attention to their ears.) Faeces are a good indication of condition. They should be dark brown and solid. Avoid any stock with chronic diarrhoea. Look at and handle all of the litter. At this age, they may well still be nibbling at fingers but should not attack your hand. Examine them for sores, runny eyes and dirty ears. Avoid any stock that is not one hundred per cent fit.

Talk to the breeder. Do not make the mistake of trying to pretend that you are an expert and know all that there is to know about ferrets. Such bravado will often prevent a ferreter from parting with any of his stock to you. Instead, question him on the sport in general and, in particular, about his ferrets. We are all vain creatures, and we all appreciate the opportunity to sing our own praises. If you like the ferrets that you see, tell the owner. He will undoubtedly be more than pleased with such remarks. Such a compliment is worth more than gold to a true ferreter.

When it is time to discuss the cost, you may find that the breeder will ask only a very small sum, perhaps with the condition that, should he be so inclined, he can come to you in future years for some stock, again at a reasonable price. On the other hand, you may get a nasty surprise when the breeder asks you for several times the price that you had in mind. Do not be put off! I often use this ploy to see just how keen and committed any potential buyers are, before I will part with my precious stock. I also use the same ploy to rid myself of time wasters and people who I just do not feel would make suitable owners for my ferrets. If the cap fits . . .!

When you have chosen your ferrets, take them home and place them in a pre-prepared cage, complete with water and food. Remember that these youngsters will have been used to the company and play of their siblings and, when they suddenly find themselves without this, they may well be rather unsettled. For this reason, it is advisable to spend some time playing with and handling them. This will also set the scene for a healthy rapport in the future.

Handling and Taming

Good ferrets do not bite and, to my mind, there is no such thing as a bad ferret, only a bad owner. From an early age, ferret kits must be handled gently but carefully and they will soon learn that your hands are neither potential food, nor a threat. They will come to love you and look forward to your handling them. Never, during all of the time that I have been involved with ferrets, have I been seriously bitten. On the few occasions that a ferret has nipped me, it has always been due to my own clumsiness.

I handle my young stock while they are still in the nest. At this age I expect to have my fingers nibbled but, as the ferrets are so young and weak, this is not a painful experience.

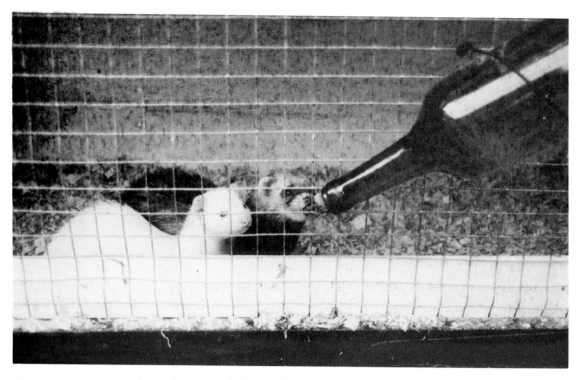

Ferrets are gregarious animals and should never be kept on their own.

Nevertheless, the youngsters need to be taught that your fingers are not on the menu, and I do this by gently tapping their noses every time that they try to bite me. They soon learn. All of the time that I am handling them, I keep up a constant soft conversation with them. I believe that the voice is just as important as the hands and can be used to calm and reassure ferrets of any age. Talking to small, furry animals does give rise to strange looks from the neighbours, though!

The next step is for me to dip my fingers into a mixture of milk and egg. I then offer my fingers to the youngsters to lick. Again, if they try to bite me, they receive a gentle tap on the side of their nose. Within a very short time, they are entirely trustworthy. Keep all movements steady and smooth; if you make sudden, unexpected and/or jerky movements, the ferret may nip you through fear. If that happens, you cannot blame the ferret, only yourself.

When picking up ferrets, place one hand around the torso, with the thumb and first finger around the neck and the other hand under the backside, to take the animal's weight. It is also possible to pick up a ferret by lifting it with the 'elbows' of the front legs. At first, all ferrets that are unused to being handled will struggle and try to escape from the hands holding them. At such times, do not increase the pressure on the ferret's body to try to prevent her from moving, as this may well cause injury to the ferret. Instead, allow the ferret to move around on your hands and arms, keeping a careful eye on her, in case the ferret loses her balance or footing. While holding her in your arms, give the animal a titbit, perhaps in the shape of a small piece of meat. This is a very good way to win the ferret's confidence and get it to accept you – the beginnings of a good relationship and a good rapport.

Training

A lot has been written about the need to train a ferret to do its job correctly. Some books devote huge sections to this aspect of ferreting. To my mind, there is no need to teach an animal to carry out a perfectly natural function. The ferret is, by nature, a hunting animal and, left to her own devices, she will do the job naturally. Undoubtedly, the best way for a young ferret to learn its trade is to follow the example of an experienced ferret but, if you do not possess such an animal, do not despair.

Most animals have an instinctive fear of the unknown and, for this reason, some young ferrets may be reluctant to enter a dark tunnel which heads down almost vertically. Choose instead a reasonably sized tunnel in a burrow that you know is uninhabited and consists of no more than two or three holes. Ensure that the tunnel – initially at least – slopes slightly upwards, and place the ferret just in the mouth of the tunnel. Do not worry if she pauses and sniffs the air for a time before venturing into the abyss, this is perfectly natural. Do not try to force her underground before she is ready; to do so may cause the ferret to fear the underground world, thus rendering her virtually useless for hunting. Be patient.

After one or two outings of this nature, take the tyro to a small burrow where you would expect to find a rabbit or two and enter her. Once she has had her first encounter with rabbits, there will be no stopping her! Remember that she will be very excited when she comes out and so do not try to pick her up before she has completely left the hole. To do so will encourage her to 'skulk', i.e. always wait just inside the entrance to a tunnel and move away from your hand every time that you try to pick her up. It is easier to start this habit than it is to stop it!

By the time that your ferret has entered occupied rabbit holes a few times, she will be fully 'trained' and, in future, whenever you take the ferret out of her cage to put her into a carrying box, she will realise that she is probably going hunting, and may even tremble with excitement. This excitement will always be evident when the ferret is taken out of the carrying box on site and introduced to the opening in the ground from which exudes the unmistakable aroma of rabbit! Your ferrets will look forward to such outings and consider them in exactly the same way that we do – not work but good, clean fun with (hopefully) a good meal of rabbit flesh at the end of the day.

3

Housing

'Home is home, though it be homely.'
English Proverb

Ferrets have been kept successfully in many different types of cage, many of which are totally unsuitable – a fact which says a lot for the ferret, but very little for the many thoughtless owners who cannot be bothered to find out a little about the needs of their charges, let alone ensure that the animals have a comfortable and healthy life. All cages for ferrets must be totally weather-proof, giving shelter from both the cold and the heat – damp and draughts are two of the biggest killers of captive animals – and should be large enough for the inhabitants to lead a 'normal' life, allowing them to exercise and play.

By nature, ferrets are extremely clean animals and will habitually use the same area as a toilet – usually the corner furthest from their sleeping area. Some cage designs take advantage of this habit, removing the solid floor from the toilet corner and replacing it with wire mesh. This can be advantageous as it will allow both the urine and the faeces to drop out of the cage, thereby lessening the risk of the ferrets' fur becoming soiled. To me, it causes too many other problems to make it worthwhile and, in a multi-storey cage unit, it is obviously completely impractical.

Some ferret keepers prefer to have all of the floor made of wire mesh but I have never held with this practice and so cannot recommend it. A wire floor will allow cold and draughts into the cage and, again, in multi-storey units, it is totally impractical. Wire floors were originally fitted to help ensure that the inmates did not have to spend all of their waking hours walking on wet, dirty floors. At that time, it was believed that foot rot was the result of such conditions. If owners cannot be bothered

to keep the floors of their ferrets' cubs reasonably clean and dry, then they should not keep ferrets (or any other animal for that matter).

Traditionally, there are two main types of ferret cage – the 'cub' and the 'court'.

Ferret Cubs

The ferret cub is very similar to a traditional rabbit hutch. However, ferrets are born escapologists and far stronger and more intelligent than rabbits, and it is necessary to provide accommodation that reflects these considerations. The following are, therefore, minimum standards only.

To house two ferrets (the minimum number that should be kept), the cub must be at least 1.5m (5ft) long, 0.5m (2ft) high and 0.5m (2ft) deep; the nest box area (sleeping quarters) must be at least a quarter of the total volume of the cub, and should have a separate door through which you can gain direct access. The ferrets' entrance/exit from the main area to and from the sleeping area, should consist of an opening approximately 7.5 × 7.5cm (3 × 3in), raised about 7.5cm (3in) from the floor of the cub. You should be able to open all doors and the roof for routine cleaning and maintenance. Ensure that some form of holding device is fitted for the roof since, as ferrets are extremely inquisitive and do climb, a roof which is suddenly blown down can be lethal.

It is possible to build two or more cubs, one above the other. This is particularly useful if space is limited and extra cubs are needed – for separating hob and jill at breeding time, for instance.

A typical ferret cub.

A two-storey ferret cub.

The body of the cub should be built from good quality hard wood, at least 2cm (1in) thick. The joints should be such that no draught or rain can enter. While it is not necessary to go to the lengths of dovetailing the joints, it is recommended that any small cracks are filled with a proprietary brand of non-poisonous filler – *never* use putty, as this is toxic. All doors must be well fitting and secured not only to prevent the ferrets themselves from escaping, but also to prevent humans from stealing or interfering with the animals. The wire netting used must be of the welded mesh type, as normal 'rabbit mesh' is not strong enough to withstand the rigours of the ferrets' continual assault. This wire mesh should be at least 16swg and have a mesh size of either 2.5×2.5cm (1×1in) or 2.5×1cm (1×0.5in).

In order to ensure a long, maintenance-free life for the cub, several coats of good quality non-toxic gloss paint should be applied to the inside. I prefer to use a light coloured paint as this gives a good finish and also provides the inhabitants with a nice cheery home. The outside of the cub should be treated with a top quality wood preserver. Ensure that the preserver is non-toxic and never use creosote.

Gloss paint will serve the purpose of protecting the timber but the roof is best covered with heavy-duty roofing felt. It is worthwhile to fit a sloping roof (about 5cm (2in) higher at the back than at the front), as this will allow water to run off easily, thereby preventing puddles building up. The roof should also extend about 5cm (2in) beyond the front of the cub, thus preventing the water from dripping into the cub. Looked after properly, such a cub will last for many years; one of my own cubs is now over fifteen years old and still going strong.

A good covering of wood shavings on the floor of the cub will help to keep the interior reasonably clean, soaking up urine and other fluids which will find their way on to the floor. Do not use saw dust, as this has a nasty habit of going up the ferrets' noses or in their eyes, sometimes with dire consequences. A good supply of shavings should also be placed in the bottom of the nest box and, in the winter, plenty of good quality, soft meadow hay. Do not provide too much hay in the summer, as this will cause the ferrets to overheat. Do not be surprised if, during an uncharacteristically warm British summer, the ferrets carry all of the hay out of their nest box. Ferrets are highly intelligent and know how to adjust the temperature in their sleeping quarters.

Cubs are best raised about 15 to 20cm (6 to 8in) off the ground, to prevent damp and cold from striking upwards and also to save one's back! This can easily be achieved with a few house bricks, although it may make the structure rather unstable. It is better to take the time and effort and equip the cage with proper legs. However, care must be taken with multi-storey cub units, as they can all too easily be blown over in a sudden gust of wind, or even simply topple over with the movement of the inmates. Such units should either be firmly anchored to a sturdy wall or building, or be secured to several strong stakes, driven into the ground and extending up the sides.

The area that cubs stand on is best covered with either concrete or well-laid paving slabs. This will ensure that one corner of the cub does not sink into the ground, causing it to topple over. It is also worth investing in a proper path to the cub area, again made of either concrete or paving slabs. The benefit of this path will be realised during the first winter, when the rain and snow will turn any other type of path into a sea of mud.

Ferret Courts

The ferret court is similar to an aviary, with a few minor alterations and more security. In order to ease the day-to-day burdens, it should be high enough to allow easy access to the owner, via a well fitting door. The ferrets will take advantage of this extra height for exercising, for although many authorities will tell you that ferrets do not climb, they do. Visitors have asked if mine are related to monkeys!

The court itself should be set on concrete, for ease of cleaning and also to prevent the ferrets from digging their way out. Floors made from paving slabs are not entirely satisfactory since, unless the gaps between the slabs are filled with either a cement or concrete mixture, they will harbour germs and allow plants (some of which may be poisonous) to grow. Natural earth floors quickly become a sea of mud in wet weather and are almost impossible to keep clean.

A good size for a court to house between three and six ferrets is 2 × 2 × 2m (6.5 × 6.5 × 6.5ft). The frame can be made of timber or metal; again, it is recommended that, whatever material is used, it is treated to protect it against the rigours of the British climate. It must be strong and securely fastened to the concrete base before the wire netting is attached. As with the cub, this should be of the welded mesh type, at least 16swg and with a mesh size of either 2.5 × 2.5cm (1 × 1in) or 2.5 × 1cm (1 × 0.5in). Ensure that the mesh is attached to the frame securely by fixing a staple at least every 7cm along the frame. To prevent any escapes and the unwelcome incursions of vermin the wire mesh should either be embedded into the concrete or extended down into the ground to a depth of at least 30cm (1ft). This will dissuade the ferrets from trying to dig an escape route, but even so, it must be checked regularly.

Ferret courts come in two main types: one consists of a small building, usually like a small wooden garden hut, attached to a wire run, while the other style consists entirely of a wire run containing one or more nest boxes for the inhabitants. I personally prefer the first type.

Access can be gained via a door in the wire mesh run in both types. In the first type, the door to the wooden building opens from the run area. This ensures that the ferrets cannot escape undetected while one is entering the building. This building also has one or more ferret-sized entrances, to facilitate the ferrets' comings and goings, without letting in too much cold air. These entrance holes should be at least 30cm (1ft) above the ground. Small wooden ramps (not ladders) should be securely fastened into position, both inside and outside the building to enable the ferrets to come and go easily. These should be fitted with crosspieces around every 2.5cm (1in), to help the ferrets climb them. (Do not make the ramps at too steep an angle – 30 degrees is about the optimum).

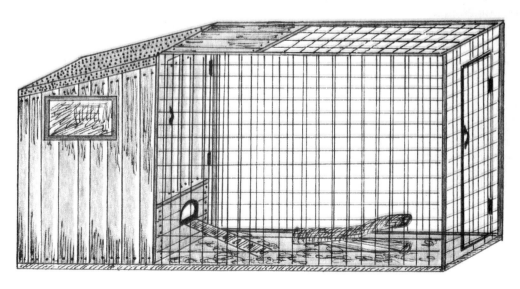

A ferret court.

Nest boxes should all have opening lids, as well as small entrances for the ferrets.

The wooden building may contain one or more separate nest boxes, or have a few shelves fixed about 20cm (8in) above the ground. These shelves should have small lips, about 2.5cm (1in) high, all the way around and also have wooden ramps firmly fixed in place for the ferrets to climb on and off.

In the second type, I like to see part of the roof of a court covered over, to give the inhabitants shelter from the elements and shade from the heat of the summer sun. A piece of marine quality ply wood, suitably treated and fixed across one end of the court, will suffice. It is also worth considering making at least one of the walls (the one facing prevailing winds) of solid material, thus acting as a wind break and general protection against the elements.

Several nest boxes, each about 45 × 45 × 30cm (1.5 × 1.5 × 1ft) should be raised approximately 15cm (6in) off the ground, fitted with ramps, and positioned around the court. I like to have opening roofs on these next boxes, so that I can check on any litters. Place a good covering of wood shavings in the bottom of each nest box and ensure that there is an adequate supply of top quality meadow hay within the court. The ferrets will gather this and place quantities in their own nest box as and when they need it. Remember that more hay will be needed in very cold weather, and far less in warm weather. It is always better to supply too much than not enough bedding, leaving the ferrets to make their own beds according to the prevailing weather conditions.

The inside of a court can be supplied with various items, such as branches, plants or bushes in tubs or even a rockery. These items will not only enhance the appearance of the court to human eyes, they will also provide play items for the ferrets. Always ensure that any plants placed inside a court are not poisonous to the ferrets, and that all other materials used are safe too.

Positioning

Whatever type of cage is chosen, it is vitally important that the site is carefully considered before its construction. Remember that the cage's inmates cannot move from that area and are, therefore, quite literally at the mercy of the elements. The chosen site must provide shelter from wind, rain, sun, heat and cold – a tall order.

I cannot give exact rules on where one should or should not position a cub or court, as every piece of land/garden is so different. When making your choice, however, there are certain factors to be considered. Remember that, in the cold weather, some sunshine will be extremely useful to keep the ferrets warm but, in the summer, that same sunshine could prove fatal. Also remember that the sun moves throughout the day; take advantage of this fact. Early morning sun is much cooler than that of midday and it is usually possible to position the cage so that the inmates benefit from an early morning sun bathing session but do not cook in the midday heat. In extremely hot periods, a wet sack (kept damp) hung over the cage will usually keep the temperature down to manageable levels.

Ascertain the direction of the prevailing wind (which will, of course, drive the rain) and ensure that there is an adequate and effective windbreak. A piece of exterior, or marine quality plywood will make an excellent windbreak. So too will a trellis covered with a non-poisonous creeping plant. This will also look far better.

Cleaning

I am a great believer in making life as simple as possible, and this philosophy is very important when it comes to the day-to-day maintenance/ cleaning of the ferrets' quarters. While it is obvious that the housing should be of a design enabling the inmates to lead a relatively normal life, it should also be borne in mind that, if the design does not facilitate easy – and thorough – cleaning, then you will probably be less inclined to carry out that task, thus preventing the ferrets from leading the happy existence that they deserve.

Also remember that ferrets do have a characteristic smell and that your neighbours may not share your enthusiasm. Good, friendly neighbours are very difficult to find, and bad smells drifting over the garden fence may not be conducive to good relations!

With this in mind, ensure that the cage has no nooks or crannies where dirt (and therefore germs) can accumulate. If the interior is made as flush as possible, cleaning will not become a chore that you will seek to avoid. As discussed in Chapter 11, ferrets which are kept in clean, dry and draught free conditions are usually very healthy; prevention is better (and usually cheaper) than cure.

Whether a cub or a court is used to house your ferrets, thorough cleaning should take place at least once a week. Start by removing the ferrets and placing them in a secure box or spare cage. It is all too easy to concentrate on the cleaning tasks and forget that the ferrets are free to escape if they so wish. Once they are secure, remove all the wood shavings and hay, placing this in a plastic bag, which will be disposed of, preferably by burning. Storing large quantities of rubbish will lead to smells and possible health hazards.

Next, using a hand brush with hard bristles, brush out the interior, ensuring that no corner is overlooked. When completely clean, wipe the surface with a mild solution of bleach and water. This will kill off all the germs and also ensure that the cage does not smell – ferret urine has a nasty habit of seeping into wood, unless it is well treated/painted. Before replacing the shavings and hay with fresh supplies, wipe out the whole of the cage with neat disinfectant. Do not use any disinfectant that turns white in water, as this usually indicates that it contains phenol, which can cause illnesses in ferrets. If there are areas where the dirt will not simply wash off, use a scraper or pan scrubber. I find that one of the best instruments for the job is a paint scraper.

Do not skimp with the shavings; ensure that

there is a covering of about 3 to 4 cm (1 to 2in) all over the floor. I find it useful to put a 'baffle' across the bottom of the wire door on my cubs to prevent the shavings from being pushed out. This is also useful to reduce draughts in cold weather and prevent ferret kits from crawling through the wire mesh. If the ferrets remove some of the hay from their nest box when they are returned to their cage, do not worry; it is their way of telling you that they are too warm. Simply remove the excess to prevent it from becoming fouled.

Shavings are not necessary in ferret courts, but may be used to advantage in the ferrets' toilet corner, where they will soak up urine and dry out faeces, facilitating their easy removal, and thus keeping smells to the minimum. Make provision for fastening a water bottle to the outside of the cage. This is far preferable to the traditional dish as the water in a dish may soon become fouled and undrinkable, even if the dish is emptied, cleaned and replenished daily. Use a stainless steel spout on

the bottle and check it daily, in case it has become blocked. A bottle made from dark coloured glass will inhibit the growth of algae on the inside of the bottle which, as well as being a possible health risk, is extremely unsightly. During periods of very low temperatures, the water in the bottles may well freeze. Sometimes this freezing causes the glass bottle to crack or even completely smash, with the attendant problems of both lack of water for the ferrets and a possibility of injury to them. Covering the bottles with insulating material designed for water pipes, is a good way of preventing this and is to be recommended in periods of intense cold. Food dishes should be large, heavy and easy to clean.

A useful tip to reduce the risk of smells and generally improve upon the cleaning regime, is to have two buckets by the door of the cage, one containing a mild solution of disinfectant, the other fresh water. These should be cleaned out and replenished at regular intervals, particularly during warm weather. As the dirty

Two useful cleaning utensils, both available from decorating shops.

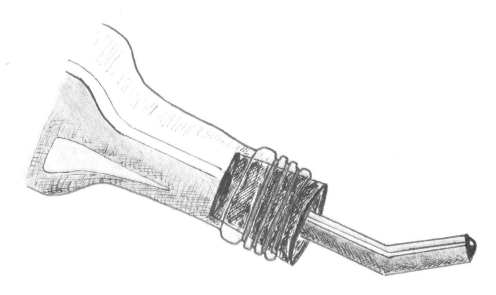

A drinking bottle, showing stainless steel spout.

The use of coloured glass bottles will help to prevent the accumulation of algae.

feeding bowls are removed, they can be washed and rinsed in the buckets, thus lessening the risk of smell and/or disease.

Flies are always a nuisance in warm weather, and they are best tackled by keeping to a strict cleaning regime, regularly clearing the toilet area, and by suspending fly papers around the outside of the cage. Ferrets are natural hoarders and particular attention should be paid to any left-over food, which the ferrets may well hide away in a corner of the cage (usually, but not always, in the nest box). In warm weather, maggots will appear within a few days unless the cage is kept scrupulously clean and all the surplus food removed regularly. Never use insecticidal sprays while the cage is inhabited.

Security

There will always be some people who, for various reasons, will attempt to interfere with or steal your property, whether this be your hi-fi or your ferrets. I cannot tell you how to protect the hi-fi, nor can I offer a foolproof and infallible method of preventing unauthorised access to your ferrets. However, in order to make it as difficult as possible for the would-be thief, I always use good quality padlocks and hasps on all my ferret cubs and courts. These are fixed on to the frame not with screws, but with nuts and bolts, which are then soldered or brazed to further secure them. True, these will not prevent someone from cutting through the wire, but they will slow them down and are likely to deter all but the most determined thief.

If you use self-locking padlocks, always ensure that you have at least one spare key, preferably where you can easily find it! In order to protect the padlocks from the weather, treat them regularly with a water repellent. A piece of old inner tube, pinned over the lock as a flap, will keep most rain off, thus lengthening the useful life of the padlocks.

4

Feeding

'There is no love sincerer than the love of food.'
George Bernard Shaw

Ferrets are carnivores and, as such, their natural diet is one of flesh, i.e. whole carcasses of mammals, birds, reptiles, fish, amphibians and even some invertebrates. This may seem obvious, and yet many ferreters have' (often reasonably successfully), kept their ferrets on a diet of bread and milk.

The main components of any diet are proteins, carbohydrates, vitamins, fats, fibre and minerals.

Protein

Proteins are essential for growth and tissue maintenance and should form at least twenty per cent of the ferrets' diet. They are present in meat, eggs and milk. Although there are many different proteins, all consisting of different arrangements of about twenty amino acids, it is not necessary to differentiate between them here. It should be obvious that, while all ferrets require a high protein diet, this is even more important when considering nursing mothers, their kits and young ferrets in general.

Carbohydrates

Carbohydrates provide the body with heat and material for growth. As they are made up of carbon, hydrogen and oxygen (which combine to form cellulose, starch and sugar), excess amounts are stored as fat in the body, often leading to obesity. This can cause medical problems and difficulties in breeding.

Vitamins

There are five main vitamins which concern us – A, B, C, D, and E. All are essential to ferrets, and a deficiency can be detrimental to the ferrets' health.

Vitamin A   Found in milk, eggs, liver and fish-liver oils, and in some other foods (such as vegetables) which do not concern us here; a lack of this vitamin can cause poor growth, diarrhoea, poor eyesight and skin complaints.
Vitamin B   Found in meat, milk and fish and, again, in other foods which do not concern us; vitamin B deficiency can cause lack of appetite, diarrhoea, dermatitis, poor growth and nervous disorders.
Vitamin C   Found in fruit and vegetables; this vitamin appears to be necessary for ferrets only in small quantities.
Vitamin D   Found in dairy products (including eggs), fish-liver oils and liver; without it your ferrets will not grow the strong teeth and bones that are essential for their well-being. (Rickets is caused by a lack of vitamin D.)
Vitamin E   Found in eggs (the yolk) and certain vegetable oils; a lack of this vitamin can cause infertility, heart and circulation problems and skin complaints.

Fats

Fat provides the ferret's body with energy but given too much, the body will store it in the tissue. This can lead to many problems, including mating difficulties and heart problems.

Fibre

Fibre (or roughage, as it used to be called) is essential for the well-being of the ferret's digestive system. Fibre will keep the ferret 'regular' and this will help prevent many of the diseases – including cancer of the bowel – with which some ferrets are afflicted. The ferret finds fibre in the fur, feathers and gut contents of her prey.

Minerals

Minerals, in very small amounts, are necessary for all animal life but as they are contained in almost all the foods that are likely to be fed to ferrets, their specific roles and sources need not concern us unduly; except that is, for calcium. This is essential for the ferret's health, as it enables the animal to grow strong bones and teeth. Calcium is to be found in the bones and teeth of all animals, as well as in milk.

As you can see, most of the constituents of a balanced diet for the ferret can be supplied by feeding whole carcasses. As this is the natural diet of the ferret's wild cousin, the polecat, this should come as no surprise. This does not mean that the complete carcass of a dead rabbit should be thrown in to the ferrets' cage and left until it is all eaten. Such practices are bad husbandry and will, eventually, lead to illness and possibly the death of one or more of your ferrets. Rabbits should be cut into portions of various sizes, all with the fur left on. The guts, too, can be fed to ferrets, providing that they have been inspected for such diseases as liver fluke (visible as white dots on the infected animal's liver).

Unless one has the opportunity and good fortune to have access to large areas of land – and the animals and birds that live there – this kind of diet is often impossible to supply. Do not despair! There are acceptable alternatives. Road casualties are often a good source of food for the captive ferret. On most journeys

through the British countryside an alert driver will spot many dead animals by the roadside. These are usually rabbits or pigeons, with the occasional song bird or rodent. All of these can be fed to ferrets, providing that a few precautions are observed. However, wild rodents should not be fed unless you can be sure that they are free from disease and, even then, they should be thoroughly gutted and inspected before feeding. As the risks of infection are so great, I would not recommend their feeding to ferrets.

Many road casualties are young animals, who have not had the chance to learn of the dangers of the world. These, of course, are ideal to feed to the ferrets. It is the older ones that you should be wary of, as they were perhaps too sick or injured to avoid the cars on the road. As such, they should not be fed to your stock. Never feed old meat either, i.e. from bodies that have been on the roadside for more than a few hours. The flesh of these animals or birds may already be infected with the *Clostridium botulinum* bacteria, the cause of botulism. In almost all cases, this disease proves fatal to ferrets. Check the body for signs of illness – puffy eyes, festering sores and/or poor fur, skin or feathers – and discard any that are suspect.

Friends and farmers who shoot can often be relied upon to provide the occasional (and sometimes regular) pigeon, corvid or rabbit and, of course, one's own catch from rabbitting can also be utilised. These will, however, not be enough to provide all the food for your ferrets; a regular supply of good quality food is required for the animals' well-being.

Dog Food

A ready supply of quality meat is always available from the supermarket, in the shape of tinned dog and cat food. Many ferreters use this as a basis for their ferrets' diet and, to a certain extent, this will suffice. One of the more widely used brands has a high cereal content, which is surprising as ferrets do not normally eat cereals. Personally, I use tinned pet foods containing all meat or fish. Various brands of cat food are also widely fed, many of them containing a high fish content. Ferrets love fish.

However, some tinned foods are rather low in protein and, if you are feeding these brands, it will be necessary to supplement the feeding with either other protein-rich foods, food supplements or both. If in doubt, consult your local veterinary surgeon who will be able to offer you sound advice as well as provide the necessary supplements, if they are required. It is also recommended that tinned dog and cat food be supplemented with bonemeal powder, to ensure that the ferrets receive adequate amounts of calcium.

Many pet shops now sell slabs of 'pet meat' or brawn, of different flavours (rabbit, chicken, beef, etc.) Many of these brands are quite suitable and I like to give all of my animals variations in their diet. There is absolutely no truth in the old wives' tale that ferrets fed on rabbit meat will be more inclined to kill, rather than chase out the rabbits.

Dry Foods

The modern trend in animal nutrition is to feed 'complete diets'. These are usually either in pellet or 'muesli' form. The original idea started in zoos where they needed to be able to supply a wide range of animals with all their nutritional requirements, but found it almost impossible to do so by feeding natural foods, many of which were just not available in Britain on a regular basis. It was highly successful and it was not long before the pet trade took an interest in the idea. At first, the idea of feeding one's dog or cat with pellets or 'porridge' caused many people to avoid such foods but, eventually, the public were persuaded to give it a try and they soon discovered the merits of these foods. They are very convenient, have very little smell, are acceptable to all but the most pampered pooch, really are a 'complete diet' and are relatively

cheap. Add to that the fact that tinned pet foods contain a lot of water and it will be seen that they are definitely worth a try.

The best types for the ferret are those marketed for cats. Some of these are designed to be fed dry, while others are designed to be mixed with water before feeding. Whichever is used, a constant supply of clean drinking water is essential. Some complete foods contain a very high proportion of cereal and these should be avoided, as they are unnatural for the ferret. Semi-moist foods are high in protein and contain meat products, extra bonemeal and added vitamins and minerals; they also have the advantage of keeping the ferrets' faeces relatively firm, thus also reducing the smell.

Chicken

About ten years ago, I moved to a small village in a new area and found myself in the position of having sixteen ferrets and no ferreting! Not only did this mean that I was deprived of my favourite sport, it also meant that I had to find an alternative supply of food for the ferrets. As twelve of my ferrets were jills, and all of them pregnant, I had to find a good, reliable (and cheap!) source of food without delay. Kits never seem to have full tummies and the prospect of having to fork out vast sums of money to feed between eighty and a hundred ferrets certainly acted as a good incentive.

I visited the nearest shopping centre and found a delicatessen which sold roast chickens. A brief conversation with the shop's manager ensued and I was told that all of the chickens arrived at the shop complete with their giblets, and that these were then removed and discarded, as very few customers wanted them, even in uncooked chickens. At this, I offered to pick up and remove all of these unwanted giblets on a regular basis and the manager eagerly accepted my offer, telling me that I was doing him a great favour! It seems that the shop had received several complaints about smells, caused by the decomposing giblets, especially during the warm weather. My problem was solved. I thanked him and made sure that I always collected the giblets on a regular basis, even though on many occasions I did not need them. On these occasions, they were simply burned in the garden incinerator.

Such opportunities exist for many people and I can recommend that they be grabbed with both hands, as feeding quickly ceases to be a problem. It is important that, once you have agreed to remove the waste giblets, you do so regularly, otherwise the manager will give up saving them, and you will have to find another source.

Chicken giblets provide almost all of the constituents of a balanced diet for ferrets. The meat will contain protein, fat, carbohydrate, vitamins and minerals, while the neck complete with bones, will supply fibre and calcium. The few feathers which are often left on the necks will also provide fibre. However, take care not to feed capons to your ferrets. Capons are birds which are chemically sterilised and, by feeding such birds (or parts of them) to your ferrets, you may make the ferrets sterile too! There is also some evidence that the hormones contained in these birds can cause congenital deformities in ferrets.

When chicken farms hatch out their eggs, the young chicks are sexed at one day. All male chicks are killed, as they are considered worthless to the farmer since they obviously cannot produce eggs. At one time, these cadavers were ploughed into the soil to act as fertilisers but nowadays, with farmers (and others) trying to ensure that nothing is wasted and anything that can be sold is sold, these dead chicks are often offered for sale. Although this service was originally meant for the owners of hawks, owls and other raptors, the chicks are also eminently suitable for feeding to ferrets. As they are covered with feathers and have not been filleted, they are an excellent source of protein, fibre and calcium. They are also quite cheap to buy. Looking in the advertising pages of specialist bird magazines (such as *Cage and Aviary Bird*) will put you in touch with suppliers.

Poultry is easily infected with harmful bacteria, and is frequently blamed for outbreaks of food poisoning. Great care should be taken in feeding it to one's stock. All frozen meats should be thoroughly defrosted before feeding and fed as soon as possible. Never re-freeze defrosted meat. This will help to ensure that such ailments as botulism do not affect your stock. If you are not sure about any meat, especially chicken, boil it for about fifteen minutes before feeding it to your ferrets.

Other Foods

Raw green tripe is one of the best foods for most carnivores kept in captivity. This is usually easily obtainable, many pet shops now selling it in tubes, minced, frozen and even in tins. It does, unfortunately, have a very strong and disagreeable smell and many people will not feed it for this reason. Ferrets, however, are not deterred by this. They love green tripe. As with all other meats, ensure that the tripe is fresh and, if frozen, defrost thoroughly prior to feeding it.

Such meat as heart, lights (lungs) and udder can be bought reasonably cheaply and makes good ferret food. Although liver is enjoyed by ferrets and also contains much nutritional value, it should not be fed in excess and never form the major part of your stocks' diet as it could be harmful. Avoid any liver sold as 'pet meat'. Much of this liver is contaminated with liver fluke; I always employ the maxim that, if meat is not fit for me to eat, it is not fit for my ferrets either!

Many butchers, supermarkets and even pet stores now market 'minced pet food'. This usually consists of many different sorts of meat minced up together and frozen, and will often include offal, fat and waste. It is an open invitation for harmful bacteria and must, therefore be fed immediately that it has been properly defrosted. If in any doubt as to its suitability, boil it for at least fifteen minutes before feeding it.

Fish, as stated earlier, is relished by ferrets

Ferrets and polecats are carnivores, but are often fed solely on milk-sops – a diet not to be recommended.

but should only be fed in limited quantities. Avoid smoked, salty and fatty fish. Occasionally, I feed my own ferrets with small pieces of cod and whiting. Any fish fed must be well filleted, as fish bones can easily become lodged in a ferret's wind pipe, often with fatal results.

Eggs are to be recommended as an occasional treat, as they contain many beneficial vitamins and are a good source of protein. Raw eggs tend to cause diarrhoea if fed too often; boiled, or even scrambled eggs are acceptable and do not seem to have this effect. One egg per week is normally adequate for an adult ferret. Pregnant and nursing jills should receive more, dependent upon how large their litter is. If feeding raw, leave the egg in its shell, intact. This will provide the ferret with some activity – and you with some entertainment, as the ferret performs all kinds of antics before finally breaking through the egg shell.

Milk Sops

Many ferret owners have kept their animals on a diet of milk sops (bread and milk) and, indeed, the ferrets seem to relish the taste, but I have never used such a diet for my animals. Milk, in limited quantities, is beneficial to ferrets, containing calcium, protein, fat and some vitamins but if given regularly, it causes diarrhoea. This is certainly not good for the ferrets. Ferrets fed on a good, balanced 'natural' diet will have solid, dark faeces; those fed on milk sops will have light coloured, sloppy (and very smelly) droppings.

A diet of milk sops cannot be described as natural and, with very few exceptions, I would strongly advise against such a diet. Those exceptions are when the ferret is off her food (perhaps through illness) or as a warm treat after, or during, a very cold hunting foray. In this way, milk sops are an infrequent treat and not the basis of the ferrets' diet.

Food Quantities

Ferrets must be fed daily (although I never feed my stock on Sundays – a day of fast is good for all animals, particularly carnivores, as it helps to cleanse the digestive system), but it is almost impossible to categorically state an exact amount of food that an individual ferret should be fed.

A good rule of thumb is to feed an amount that you think is correct and then check about an hour later. If all of the food is gone (remember that ferrets are hoarders so check the cage for hidden food), feed a little extra next time until you find that, after one hour, there is still a little food left. By doing this, although slightly wasteful, you will ensure that all of the ferrets obtain sufficient food. All left overs must be removed at the end of each day.

The ferret's digestive system is quite short and, if the animal is fed too large a quantity of food, much of it will pass through the ferret undigested. For this reason, and others, it is not satisfactory merely to feed the ferrets with one large meal every couple of days. Like most animals, they will appreciate regular (daily), smaller meals, which will result in less waste, less opportunity for the food to go off before the ferrets have a chance to eat it and, consequently, less illness among the ferrets. All of this adds up to happier and healthier ferrets, not to mention happier owners, since there will be fewer visits to the local veterinary surgeon.

In very warm weather, I feed my stock in the evening, when it is cooler. This helps prevent the food from going off before the ferrets have had a chance to eat it. All left overs must be removed from the ferrets' cub or court within a couple of hours, especially in warm weather.

Water

Clean, fresh water must *always* be available to the ferrets. This is best delivered in a drinking bottle – many pet shops sell 'rabbit drinking bottles', which are ideal. A daily check should

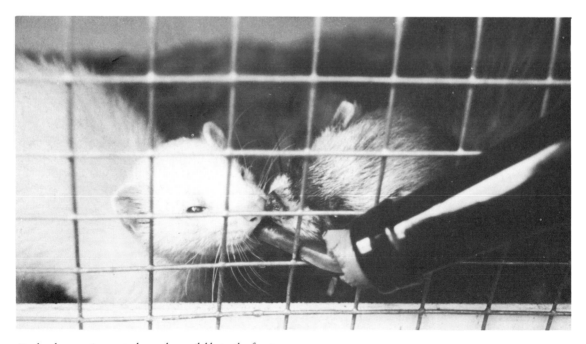

Fresh, clean water must always be available to the ferrets.

be made to ensure that the water flows freely, since the spout can easily become blocked with wood shavings, hay and even fur. Ensure that the bottle is securely fastened to the cage, on the outside. Water is even more important to ferrets fed on a dry or semi-moist diet.

Variety really is the spice of life and whatever diet you decide to feed your stock on, vary it from time to time. This will keep the ferrets happy and they will return the favour by working even better. Remember that a well thought-out and balanced diet will probably mean that your ferrets remain free from many illnesses throughout their lives. This is good for the ferrets but also good for you, as it will mean less hassle and fewer vets' bills.

5

Breeding

'The deed involves sacrifice and risk.'
Martin Buber

Sooner or later almost every ferret owner decides to breed from his (or her) stock. Indeed, there are reasons why jills should be mated every year (*see* page 46). However, this in itself is not reason enough to embark on breeding. There must always be a sound reason, otherwise the action should not be taken. The most common reason is to ensure that a particular trait, or a number of traits, in certain ferrets are not lost. These traits are usually associated with working ability and ease of handling or just plain character. An old stock man's saying is to 'put the best to the best and hope for the best'! This should never be forgotten, since it contains a lot of truth. Only the very best animals – those that are exceptional – should be bred from, and even this will not necessarily guarantee success.

Records

Accurate and detailed records are essential if one is to build up a good 'line' (strain) of any animal, and ferrets are no exception. Dates of birth, details of illness and injury, number and

A litter of young kits.

sex of progeny and both good and bad traits are just some of the information that the wise ferret keeper will record. Card indexes, loose-leaf folders and even computers can all be utilised for record keeping; the important thing is to ensure their accuracy.

There are two main methods of breeding any animals: inbreeding and line breeding.

Inbreeding

In its simplest form, inbreeding is the mating of brother to sister, mother to son or father to daughter. The main advantage of such a system is that the strain produced, very quickly develops fixed characteristics. The main dis-advantage is that the strain may also lose its vigour, sometimes leading to disease or breed-ing problems, and even failure to reproduce at all. Inbreeding that is both controlled and well thought-out is not detrimental to the ferrets.

Line Breeding

If two ferret owners with the same ideas of the 'perfect ferret' each breed their own animals from a common stock, these are known as 'lines'. Within these lines, matings are only carried out with cousins or other similarly related stock. Because both lines are from common ancestors, it is possible to intermix the lines (as and when necessary) in order to introduce 'fresh blood'; this is often known as 'hybrid vigour', since it helps to maintain the ferrets' strength and resistance to disease.

In reality, most breeders will use a combi-nation of the two methods. Personally, I will inbreed my stock for two or three years, keeping a very careful eye on their state of health and always on the lookout for any possible signs of hereditary problems, and then bring in a male from a line of common descent with my own animals. This, to my mind, gives the best of both worlds.

One of the first obvious signs of too much inbreeding in a ferret line is the appearance of a litter where one or more of the kits has a shorter than normal tail. Such animals must *not* be bred from and must never be sold into the pet market. They may well fall into the hands of someone who does not realise the dangers and is, therefore, likely to use the animal for breeding purposes. In the next year, a different male must be used as stud. This male should not be a closer relation than cousin to the jill.

Selecting Breeders

The ferrets that are to be bred should be chosen with extreme care, as the future generations will reflect the characteristics of their parents. The prospective parents should possess quali-ties that you feel are ideal. To me, those qualities are working ability, ease of handling and general good nature (though not neces-sarily in that order).

Simple Coat Colour Inheritance

Unless you are specifically trying to produce certain coat colours, this aspect should have very little influence on your choice of parents. However, if you are interested in this subject, the simple table below will supply some guide lines.

True bred poley × true bred poley = poleys
True bred albino × true bred albino = albinos
True bred poley × true bred albino = poleys*
Poleys* × true bred poleys = 25 per cent albino and 75 per cent poleys
Poleys* × poleys* = 50 per cent albino and 50 per cent poleys

Poleys* have the appearance of poleys, but they are, in fact, referred to as 'splits' or heter-zygotes, as they carry the genetic material for both poley and albino. The albino gene is masked by the dominant poley gene.

Ferrets and polecats can be born in the same litter.

In between these two extremes of colour are many shades which are known as sandies or minks – each one slightly different in colour and markings to any other. These should not be confused with moulting or older ferrets.

For those wishing to know more about coat colour inheritance in ferrets, I would advocate that they consult one of the many books on the market. For general reading on the subject of genetics, *Colour Inheritance in Small Livestock* by Roy Robinson (Fur and Feather, 1978) is to be recommended. The subject of genetics is shrouded in mystery, but the basics of coat colour inheritance (Mendelian inheritance) are quite easy for most people to grasp. All it requires is a little time and effort. Do not be put off by those who will tell you that only a genius can understand the principles involved – that is just not true.

Oestrus

When you have selected the potential parents, you must wait for the female to begin oestrus (come on heat). This occurs each year, usually in late spring. One of the main factors governing the time of oestrus is the ratio of daylight to darkness – a fact long acknowledged by laboratories and other professional breeders of small mammals. In these institutions, all of the animals live in a completely artificial environment where the hours of 'day' and 'night', along with the temperature and many other factors, are very carefully monitored and controlled. The scientific term for this response to light and dark is 'photoperiodism'.

Unless you keep your ferrets inside a building, it will be impossible for you to use photoperiodism to your advantage, so you will simply have to rely upon Mother Nature. If, however, you do keep your stock inside and also want to induce an earlier than normal oestrus, this is easily done, with no adverse effects upon the ferrets.

Both male and female ferret must be kept inside the building, as the male is dependent upon photoperiodism to make his testicles descend. The light must be controlled to give about eighteen hours of 'daylight' and six hours of 'night time' and this is best done by using one of the many household time switches that are on the market, in conjunction with one or more lamps. The light should be sufficient to emulate daylight, but not so bright that it blinds the ferrets. It will be necessary for the ferrets to be kept in such conditions for about six or eight weeks before they are duped into believing that it really is spring.

Oestrus itself is obvious. The jill's 'private parts' will become swollen and there will be traces of blood.

The Mating

The actual mating should take place in the hob's cage, if the ferrets are housed in cubs in one sex groups.

Place the jill into the hob's cage after they have both been fed a light meal, and then leave them together. Immediately the hob smells the jill, he will grab her by the scruff of the neck and drag her into his nest box. She may well squeal and appear to be fighting him; this is perfectly natural and no harm will come of it. The hob holds the jill tightly while he mates her; very often, his teeth will pierce her skin and blood will be seen on the back of the jill's neck. Again, this is no cause for concern, although I always wipe the wound with a mild antiseptic when I later separate the happy couple.

The couple should be separated and returned to their respective cages after twenty-four to forty-eight hours, where a light meal should be waiting. If the mating has been successful, the jill's vulva will dry and regain its normal size and appearance within a week to ten days. If the sexes are kept together in a court, then nature will take care of everything.

The genitalia of a jill in oestrus.

Unmated Jills

In the wild, all jill polecats will be mated at almost the first opportunity and there is a theory that, unless a ferret jill is bred from, she will die in her second season. There is some truth to this, in that, if a jill is not mated, she will remain in oestrus throughout the breeding season. This means that her vulva will remain swollen and wet for up to four months, during which time she is a prime target for all kinds of infections in her vagina and uterus, and this can often have deadly results.

Many people, however, do not want the bother of a litter of ferrets since this will mean extra work (cleaning and handling), expense (feeding and vets' fees) and the hassle of finding new homes for all of the kits. Because of this, some breeders keep a neutered hob, known as a hobble, which they are often prepared to loan to other ferret keepers. The idea is that such a neutered animal is still capable of the act of mating but, as he is sterile, the jill will not become pregnant, yet she will come out of oestrus. Your local vet or the National Ferret Welfare Society will probably be able to help you to trace the owner of a hobble, or the vet can advise on having one of your own hobs vasectomised.

The Pregnancy

Once the jill has been mated, she will require some special treatment. Although you will obviously have been feeding her a perfectly balanced diet, you must now make sure that it really *is* balanced and not lacking in any vital constituent. Your local veterinary surgeon will be able to help in this matter but, if you have been following the diet guidelines printed earlier in this book, then there should be no need to do more than continue in the same vein, but remember that she will require larger amounts of food, especially in the later stages of her pregnancy. I like to give my pregnant jills milk and eggs about twice a week. Into this I mix a little SA 37 (vitamin supplement) and

some bonemeal. Keep a careful watch on the jill's faeces and, if they appear too sloppy, cut down the milk and eggs.

The ferret's gestation period (pregnancy) is approximately forty-two days (six weeks), although my own stock have had pregnancies of anything from forty to forty-four days. Shortly before the litter is due (about seven to ten days), clean out the cage thoroughly and supply plenty of soft meadow hay, for the jill to use in nest building. If the weather is particularly warm, she may well not use any but it should always be available thoughout the period that her litter is still with her. Do not disturb her too much during this latter part of her pregnancy, but do not ignore her either. It is important that her (and your) daily routine should remain the same, in order to avoid stressing her unduly.

If more than one ferret shares the same cage, you should decide whether or not to house them separately. I feel that if the animals have enough room, as for instance in a court, it is best to leave the group together, as the jills will look after both their own and other jills' litters and keep the hob out of harm's way. Some of the kits will die when using this system, but my jills average seven to eight kits each, so there cannot be many kits that do perish.

If, however, you keep both your jills and hobs in the same cub, I would recommend that the hob is removed several weeks before the litter is due. Once the litter is born, keep a record of how many kits there are and, if the number shows a regular decrease, it is well to remove all but the nursing mother.

If a hob is around when the jill gives birth, then he may mate her again; this is called post parturition coitus and often results in a second litter.

The Birth

Ferret litters can contain up to fourteen kits, but the average litter consists of six to eight. The kits are born naked, blind and deaf and are, of course, completely dependent upon their mother for food, warmth and protection.

You will probably notice something is happening when you go to feed the jill. She will often remain in the nest box or perhaps briefly show herself at the pop hole before rushing back to her litter. Sometimes the kits can be heard crying when she leaves them, a noise that is certain to prompt her to return to the litter. Unless you know your jill very well, it is best not to disturb her for the first few days. After this time, it is quite easy to sneak a look at the litter while mum is eating or drinking. Try not to disturb the nest or to touch the kits. If you do need to touch the kits, sprinkle some of the nest wood shavings on to the litter before mum returns; this will mask your scent on the kits.

I know and trust all of my ferrets and I feel sure that the feeling is mutual. Thus, when any of my jills give birth, I am not seen as an intruder when I have a look at the nest. Even so, I do not disturb them for the sake of the exercise, as I want them to raise a happy and healthy litter. It is still true to say that I regularly handle kits from the day they are born.

My oldest jill, Izzy, never bothers when I pick up one or more of her young. She merely looks at me with a twinkle in her eye, knowing that I cannot but approve of her progeny. This exercise must not, however, be carried out with just any jill, especially one having her first litter, since she may well feel that she has to 'defend' her litter – usually by killing them. For the first few weeks of the kits' life, mum will remain with them except for forays to the food bowl or the toilet.

The kits will begin to grow fur from about day three, while their eyes will not begin to open until they are about three or four weeks old, being fully open at about five weeks. Before this time, however, they will have been crawling out of their nests, only for their mum to drag them back in by the scruff of their necks. This is a perfectly natural and harmless way for them to be carried and owners should not imagine that the jill is eating her kits.

By six weeks of age, the kits will be running riot around the cage, with their eyes and ears

Ferret kits which are handled from an early age will grow up into easily handled adults.

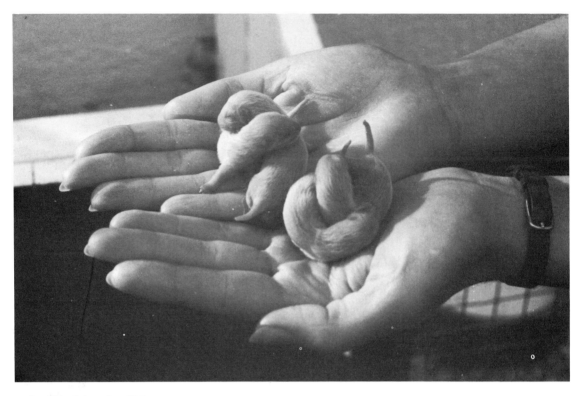

A handful of three-day-old kits.

fully functional and their fur resembling that of their parents. Mum still tries to limit their activities by constantly dragging them back to their nest but, as soon as she turns her back, out they come again! All of this activity demands energy derived from food so mum must be provided with all of the food that she (and her offspring) desire. The kits will begin eating meat at about twenty-one days of age and, from then on, they just do not seem able to find enough to eat!

Foster Mothers

Occasionally a jill will reject her litter, be unable to feed the young or even die shortly after their birth. Although it is possible to hand rear the litter it is extremely hard work, requiring your presence around the clock and, for the great majority of people, completely impractical. For the record, I raised a litter of four ferret kits from the age of two weeks. I fed them on a mixture of one part evaporated milk to two parts water, mixed with the yolk of an egg, until they were old enough to take some minced rabbit and then feed themselves. Not an exercise that I would recommend to anyone who has to get up early for work!

If you have another jill with a smallish litter, it is possible to get her to act as a foster mother to the other kits. This is best achieved by distracting mum with a full food dish and then placing the orphaned kits into the new nest. Put some of the real family on the top of the new arrivals and then sprinkle them all with nest material to mask the new arrivals' scent (and yours). This method has never failed me and I can recommend it, providing that all of the precautions outlined above are adhered to.

Kits can – and do – die before reaching maturity or even being weaned. The most

Jills spend much of their time dragging . . .

. . . and lifting their kits.

common cause is food poisoning or similar, usually brought on by lack of hygiene in the cage. It is imperative that the cage is kept as clean as possible at all times, but especially when there are young kits. Always ensure that the toilet corner is cleaned daily and that any uneaten food is removed before it has a chance to go off. (*See also* Chapter 11.)

Weaning

Providing that there is ample food available, the kits will wean themselves, becoming fully independent by the time they are eight or nine weeks old. This is the youngest age that ferret kits should ever be removed from their mother. I never allow any of my kits to go until they are at least twelve weeks old, but I have seen ferret kits of a mere four weeks offered for sale. The people who sell kits at this age do not care one iota about the animals; they are trying to make a few pounds at the expense of their ferrets. Goodness only knows what other horrors such people submit their ferrets to! There would be no point in such people offering such pitifully young animals for sale if other (sometimes well intentioned) people did not buy them. I would be quite happy to see the law changed to make such dealings a punishable offence. Ferrets deserve better!

Disposal of Surplus Stock

Assuming that all goes well with the ferrets' breeding, you will find yourself with a lot of ferrets on your hands. This may not seem like such a bad thing if you only have one jill, who gives birth to only two or three kits. However, when you have six jills, each one giving birth to seven or eight kits, the matter soon takes on more urgency! Not only do these youngsters require more space and make a lot more mess,

they also require vast amounts of food. Young ferrets seem to have insatiable appetites, and often resemble locusts in the way in which they can dispose of food.

If you have a good reputation within the ferreting world, you will find that you often have a waiting list of potential owners (all of whom you have thoroughly vetted), and this list is often greater than the number of available kits. You will also probably wish to retain one or more of the latest generation for your own use, thus insuring yourself against the future demise of any of your stock. If you are a member of the National Ferret Welfare Society, or one of its affiliated clubs, you may be able to find fellow members who will take some of your surplus stock.

Not everyone is so fortunate, and many breeders find themselves left with several unwanted kits on their hands. Although I would never recommend that anyone sell his ferrets to a complete stranger, there is often little alternative, and many ferrets are sold through the columns of local newspapers and sporting magazines. Some are also sold through the display of cards placed in gunshop windows.

If you have to resort to the latter methods of disposing of your unwanted stock, at least try to ensure that the potential buyers are suitable ferret owners. Casually interview them, telling those who are unsuitable that you have made a mistake, or that someone may be calling around tomorrow to collect the last available kit . . .! Do not sell your stock to the first person who is willing to cross your palm with silver.

If you feel that you will not be able to give all of your stock suitable homes, do not breed. Borrow (or keep yourself) a hobble, thus solving all of your problems easily. Plan for the future, and always remember that you owe your ferrets a decent life-style, in payment for all of the sport, fun and food that they supply.

6

The Rabbit

'The rabbit has a charming face: its private life is a disgrace.'
Anon

For most ferreters, the European rabbit (*Oryctolagus cuniculus*) will be the main – and in many cases the only – quarry species that is pursued. As one of the main prerequisites of a hunter is for him or her to understand the natural history of the quarry, it is appropriate that we look at the rabbit in detail.

The rabbit is, by nature, partial to open country and likes to make its home in well drained, sandy soil. Very rarely will rabbits make their home in low lying country with long grass and lush vegetation. More rabbits are to be found in areas where the weather is milder, with plenty of sunshine and winters that are not too cold. Rabbits are not too keen on rain; indeed, during heavy downpours, many rabbits drown in their burrows. Although not keen on life in coniferous woodlands, rabbits love deciduous woodland with a moderate amount of ground vegetation, the ideal environment being where this woodland is surrounded by grass and/or arable farming land. The rabbits will not go hungry, and the woodlands will provide a place for them to rest in and also to escape to, in times of danger. The rabbit does not prosper in areas of intensive agriculture or regularly cut crops.

Mild areas where there is a profusion of stone walls and hedges provide almost limitless possibilities for the rabbit to enjoy the life of Riley. A few small hillocks will also provide ample opportunity for the animals to burrow and generally set up home. One of the most popular habitats is a coastal region, in the sand dunes, where ample shelter, food and suitable land for burrowing make life relatively easy for the rabbit.

Rabbits, like ferrets, are born naked, blind and deaf and fully dependent upon their mother. The doe rabbit will make a nest from dry vegetation and line it with her own fur, which she pulls from her body, especially around her belly, thus exposing her nipples. This helps the litter of between two and eight young rabbits (kits or kittens) to feed. Weighing less than 50g (2oz), the kittens will crawl about this nest, altering their positions to help regulate their body temperatures, and to find the best feeding station. The nest itself is situated in a 'stop' – a cul-de-sac tunnel with only one entrance. This serves two purposes; one is to ensure that the nest is not in the way of – and therefore disturbed by – the other rabbits in the warren, and the other is that it is less likely to be found by predators.

The kittens develop at a very fast rate, doubling their weight by the time that they are seven days old (sometimes less). The ears open and function at about seven to eight days and the fur is clearly evident. The teeth and claws

The rabbit is the main quarry species pursued by ferreters.

Rabbits are well camouflaged . . .

. . .but their presence is easily noted from the signs of damage that they inflict.

are also visible at this age, with the eyes being fully open by about ten days of age, or earlier.

The nest is sealed up by the doe until it is time to feed her progeny. This is usually done at night, probably to help avoid predators. As they get older, the kits begin to push their way through this earth, usually emerging by the time they are between sixteen and nineteen days old. The deeper the stop, the less earth seems to be put over the nest.

By the time that the kittens are a month old, they are able to run around and indulge in play, but at this age, this is always in the vicinity of the burrow entrance. They will also graze in the same area, running back to the safety of the burrow whenever danger threatens. The mother will keep a watchful eye on her offspring during this formative period and will warn them of any danger by stamping her hind feet on the ground and raising her backside to show her 'scut' (white tail). This reaction is copied by the kittens as they head for shelter, thus proving that their emergency procedure is learned.

As the doe will have been mated about two days after giving birth to her first litter of the year, during the fourth week of the life of her first litter, mum will abandon them and give birth to yet another litter, again of between two and eight kits. She will dig another stop for the birth of this litter and the whole routine will begin again.

The first litter will now have lost its dependency on their mother and will fend for themselves. They will have already developed the habit of passing soft pellets, which are then reingested in order that the full amount of goodness can be obtained from the vegetation which forms their staple diet. Fully used to reacting to danger by running for the shelter of the burrow, during play they will develop their own hierarchy or social order, the strong rabbit pushing the weaker out of the way while in the nursery stop. Although at this stage this is still done in play, it will later develop into real aggression.

As they develop, the litter will begin to split up and move into other parts of the burrow.

The exact movements are dictated by both the size of the burrow and the size of the colony. If the burrow is large, or the colony small, then the young rabbits will take up residence in the centre or main area. If the burrow is small or the colony large, the newcomers will be forced to move to the outer areas. If the burrow is particularly crowded, young rabbits will spend much of their time sleeping outside, gaining their shelter from the long grass or other such vegetation.

At the centre of every rabbit colony is a dominant female, known as either the queen or the matriarch. Her litters have a distinct advantage over the other litters of the colony, in that they are born and brought up at the very centre of the burrow and enjoy the protection of the most powerful buck and doe in the colony. As long as the young rabbits remain submissive, they are free to continue to live in such conditions.

The traditional breeding season of the European rabbit is between May and September, but it is common to find rabbit kittens throughout almost all of the year, especially in years when the winter is quite mild. The old countryman's guide to when ferreting was permissible was 'during the months with an R'. Undoubtedly the best advice as to when to stop hunting rabbits with ferrets is when one has captured young rabbits or does in kindle (pregnant).

If the colony is too big to find sufficient food in the immediate vicinity of the burrow, then many of the young rabbits (both bucks and does) will make their way to an area where they can find sufficient food for themselves. This is sometimes miles away, although usually less. Here they will dig a new burrow and thus start a new colony. They may also join up with, or be joined by, other young rabbits. This is nature's way of limiting the extent to which a colony might become inbred. As the newly dominant doe approaches her full term of pregnancy, she begins to dig the first burrow, where she will then give birth to her litter. As she may have up to six litters in this first year, and each one will be given a new

A small bolt-hole such as this is easily overlooked.

Obvious rabbit holes, but the vegetation may well be hiding others.

Find every hole – an almost impossible task in cover such as this.

The main entrance to a burrow – well used and obvious to even the most casual observer.

Cross-section of a small rabbit burrow.

nursery, it can be seen how the burrow (and also the colony) will quickly grow. By the late summer, the colony, dominated by the matriarch, will be firmly established and will continue to grow year after year, until saturation point is achieved once more.

Myxomatosis

The rabbit is well known both for its breeding potential and for its destruction of crops. While to many members of the public the rabbit is regarded as a charming pet, a bunny, to the farmer it is, and has been for many years, regarded as a pest and to many as 'public enemy number one'! The sportsman tends to take a somewhat philosophical view on the whole matter. He appreciates that rabbits do, indeed, make excellent pets (I know many avid ferreters who love nothing more than hunting the rabbit and yet also keep pet rabbits – although they usually make the excuse that these pets are simply for the children – even though the children may have left home many years ago!) He also realises that they are a pest (the 1954 Pest Act listed them as agricultural pests, and required that farmers and other landowners must try to limit their population) which needs to be controlled in order to reduce the damage to crops.

The sportsman does not, however, believe that the whole rabbit population should be exterminated and he most certainly does not agree with the introduction of diseases such as myxomatosis. This vile disease was introduced into Britain (Kent) from France in 1953. This was, so the story goes, done deliberately in order to curtail the rapid growth of the rabbit population in Britain. Within twelve months,

Rabbit scrapes.

it is thought to have killed over sixty million rabbits, almost ninety-nine per cent of the total rabbit population of England, Scotland and Wales.

The first signs of myxomatosis are a swelling of the eyes and, usually, the ears and rectum. Within a few days, the rabbit's eyes have filled with pus, causing the animal to go blind. Within a few more days, the unfortunate beast is dead. The disease is transmitted by the flea and, since rabbits generally live in rather crowded conditions, the whole colony is quickly affected.

Myxomatosis continued to do its deadly and painful work until, in the late 1970s, it seemed to almost die out. Today there are occasional local outbreaks but, thankfully, the worst seems to be over.

Sport

When myxomatosis was at its worst, the general public, perhaps understandably, declined to eat rabbit meat and many ferrets were either destroyed or turned loose into the countryside to fend for themselves. Ferrets became rather rare creatures for many years until, with the rise once again of the British rabbit population, sportsmen began breeding and working them against the rabbit. It is true to say, however, that the British never completely regained their taste for rabbit meat, as can be seen by the price that it commands in today's market place. However, with the rise in popularity of healthy eating habits, the rabbit could, once again, become a staple of the British people.

Today's sportsmen and women who ferret for rabbits have a huge amount of respect for their quarry. Even if they were able to, they would not wish to eradicate the rabbit from

British soil. On the contrary, they wish to see the rabbit continue to live in the wild, while they harvest a sustainable crop from the population. Not only does this hunting keep the rabbit population in check, it also helps to fill a lot of stomachs with good, tasty and healthy food.

Signs of Rabbits

The signs of rabbits are obvious to anyone who walks through the countryside with open eyes; rabbit droppings and pellets can easily be seen, as can the diggings and scrapes. Crops too, show the presence of rabbits and their tell-tale destructive habits. Many young trees can be seen to have been damaged by hungry rabbits gnawing at their trunks, removing the bark over large areas of the tree. Large areas of ground are often covered with the debris of rabbits industriously digging for food.

During warmer weather, some rabbits, especially youngsters, will sit out in fields and on grassy banks. Evidence of this can be found by looking for indentations in the vegetation. Close inspection will reveal that the grass has been carefully nibbled in order to keep the 'form' to the correct shape.

7

Working

'No labour, however humble, is dishonouring.'
The Talmud

A cold, bright September morning; the sun begins its battle against the mists hanging over the countryside. The thick frost on the grass shows evidence of your movements around the entrance to the burrow and the nets that you have set look strangely out of place. Carefully lifting two jill ferrets from their box, you approach an entry hole; the jills sniff the early morning air and begin to tremble slightly with the anticipation of the hunt to come.

At the first hole, you lift the green nylon purse net slightly and place a white jill just inside the hole. The jill moves forwards a few paces and then returns to the entrance where she takes a brief look around before turning again and disappearing into the darkness below. You move over to another hole and repeat the procedure with the remaining jill – a small poley. She pauses momentarily before, with a look over her shoulders and a twitch of her whiskers, she too disappears on her underground excursion.

Some of the ingredients of good sport – ferrets in their carrying box and a bag full of purse nets.

You slowly and carefully make your way to the top of the bank, from which vantage point you can see all of the holes and their covering nets. After a few minutes, you hear a muffled thumping from under your feet; the noise is repeated – this time off to your left, in the area into which you introduced the poley. Suddenly, out of the large hole at the foot of the bank directly beneath you, a brown shape comes hurtling out of the ground and takes the purse net with it. Slightly startled by the suddenness of it, you quickly gather your senses and run towards the captured rabbit.

Grabbing the struggling animal in both hands, you place your right foot over the hole, to prevent any more rabbits from bolting before you have set the net. With a practised knock from the priest, you kill the rabbit and, placing it on the ground to the left of the hole, you remove the spare purse net that you keep in your pocket for just such an eventuality. Draping the net over the hole, you push the retaining peg into the frozen ground, just as a blur of brown and green on your left tells you that another rabbit has bolted, hitting the net and immobilising itself. Before you can move,

a third rabbit exits the burrow and makes its escape across the track and into a clump of dense foliage.

Leaping on to the rabbit struggling in the net, you curse yourself for not being quicker and push your backside over the hole while you despatch the rabbit and untangle it from the net. That done, you return to the first catch and extricate that, carefully folding and wrapping the purse net before replacing it in the pocket of your jacket. Then, with a rabbit in each hand, you climb the bank and take up position again.

Taking advantage of the apparent lull, you 'pee' the rabbits, so that their urine does not taint the meat. As you place the last rabbit by your feet, you catch sight of a white nose coming out of the hole directly below you; the albino jill has decided to come up for a breath of fresh air. Before you can move, she has turned on her heels and gone underground again – the sign of a ferret that knows her job and is determined to chase all of the bunnies from their holes.

After another ten minutes of silence, you decide to check the situation and switch on the

Rabbits leave the burrow at high speed and should be dealt with immediately.

Peeing a freshly killed rabbit.

electronic ferret detector. Sweeping it over the area, you pick up the tell-tale evidence of two ferrets still on the move and, with a sigh of relief, you decide to allow them to continue their hunt for a little while longer.

Fifteen minutes later, you are getting much too cold to stay still any longer and so you decide to call the ferrets out. Just as you reach into your pocket for the detector, a rabbit – quickly followed by a second – bolts from a hole that you had overlooked and, consequently, had not netted. Cursing loudly, you decide that you will call it a day and so you remove the car keys from your pocket to call the two workers out. The poley does not need this signal, as she was hot on the trail of the two rabbits which escaped and, stooping to pick her up, you rattle the keys to call out the albino who appears from a hole at the top of the bank, looking rather dirty after her work.

Taking both ferrets back to their carrying box, you examine them and remove any debris from their feet. Stroking each one, you tell yourself that they have certainly earned their breakfast and place them in a warm box while you paunch a rabbit and give the liver, heart and kidneys to the two ferrets who hungrily munch on the fresh meat while you begin the task of collecting in the purse nets, ensuring that the same number are collected as were set.

A typical day's ferreting will bring with it trials and tribulations but, to me, is always guaranteed to bring peace of mind. Whether the bag is one or one dozen, the joy of being out in the fresh air, soaking in the beauty of the British countryside leaves me with a sense of well-being and blocks out all of my worries. To ensure that the day also helps feed the inner man, it is essential that some planning is done beforehand.

Preparation

Time spent on preparation and planning is never wasted. A few days before ferreting an area, a detailed reconnaissance should be made. At this time, any undergrowth which might hamper operations must be removed. Look for evidence of rabbits, such as scrapes, fresh droppings or damage to trees, plants and bushes. Special attention should be given to looking for any isolated hole which can be easily over-looked on the day itself. Such holes are very often used only in emergencies and so may not look to be in use. However, if you neglect to net such a hole, Murphy's Law will become operative and every rabbit in the burrow will decide to use that hole to escape.

Check with the landowner that it will be okay for you to ferret that particular piece of his land as, if he has already made plans to use that same area, you will be wasting your time – and probably making yourself rather unpopular too.

At home, work carefully through your check-list and ensure that every item of equipment is in sound working order. Purse

Ferrets are best carried in boxes, rather than in bags.

nets must be checked for damage, and debris removed (this should have been done before they were stored). Check that the net purses easily and replace the cord if it shows signs of fraying. Carefully fold each net and wrap it securely. Electronic detectors should be checked to ensure that the batteries are in good working order. I make it a rule to change all batteries at the beginning of each season or after any prolonged period of inactivity. During storage, batteries must be removed from the equipment and stored separately. At the very least, a complete set of spare batteries should be taken on every field trip. Examine the ferret carrying box and ensure that all of the catches work and that the hinges are free moving. Place fresh wood shavings and hay in the box and make sure that the carrying strap is secure.

Once all of the items have been checked for damage etc., go through the check list again, ticking off each item as it is placed in the bag in preparation for the forthcoming hunting trip.

The Big Day

On the morning of the outing, feed the ferrets with their usual breakfast. Although some people recommend that their animals should be starved before a day's work, I feel that such action merely tempts the ferret to kill, eat and then lay-up, resulting in your having to dig the animals (and their kill), out. I have never been persuaded that digging is a field sport! I always take along a small bottle filled with milk to give to the ferrets during their working day and, if the day is to be long, I paunch a rabbit and feed them the organs to sustain them in their labours.

On arrival at the chosen site, pay a visit to the owner to remind him that you will be working in the area; that way, he will not worry about any movements, which he may otherwise have thought were those of a poacher or other unauthorised person. I also make it a rule to offer a couple of rabbits to the owner at the end of the day – after all, they are

Setting purse nets correctly . . .

his! Before leaving the car to begin work, check that you have all of the equipment with you and then, quietly, make your way to the scene of the intended action. If you are using a dog (*see* Chapter 9), ensure that it is under full control and keep it quiet; frightened rabbits will prefer to take their chances underground, rather than face a definite enemy on the surface.

When you reach the burrows, place all of the equipment safely on the ground and out of the way; it is surprising how it always manages to end up under one's feet. Always work to a system; start at one end of the burrow and count each net as you set it. Do the same at the end of the day and you will never lose a purse net. Setting purse nets is an art which will only come with experience. The nets must be free enough to purse when the rabbits enter them, but not so free that they purse of their own accord. Where two or more holes begin in the same area, each one must be covered, otherwise you are asking for trouble.

It is almost always the case that you will not

. . .requires skill, which will only come with experience.

A purse net correctly placed will almost certainly capture any rabbit bolting from this hole.

Two holes together require separate purse nets, arranged so that they do not interfere with each other.

If you make a habit of drying and neatly folding your purse nets after use, it will be easier to set them the next time.

Ensure that where two purse nets are set in close proximity, they do not hinder each other's operation.

have enough purse nets with you and, if that happens, under no circumstances should any hole be left uncovered. Bags, items of clothing and bits of rubbish can all be utilised to block a hole. It is often possible to place a carrying box over a hole, but ensure that it is well balanced, otherwise the escaping rabit may well simply push it out of the way. Push the net's peg well into the ground, without hammering it. Remember that when a rabbit breaks cover, it will do so at considerable speed and, if your pegs are not sound, you may well lose it. In very hard ground, it may be best to use metal spikes, rather than the normal wooden pegs.

Once all of the holes have been covered, return to the carrying boxes for the ferrets. I always work them in pairs, entering one into each end of the dig. When doing so, lift up the corner of the purse net and allow the ferret to walk down the hole at her own speed. Very often, the ferret will go part way down and then turn around and return to the surface. In most cases, she will then turn again and commence working. However, it is always worth while waiting for a few minutes to ensure that she is, indeed, going to go underground of her own accord.

Once both ferrets are underground, you must have patience and stay alert. Do not smoke. Rabbits have an acute sense of smell, and cigarette smoke will warn them of your presence. It is tempting to stamp one's feet to keep them warm during this time, but again, this will notify the rabbits of your presence and probably cause them to face the ferrets, resulting in a kill and your having to dig.

When the first rabbit bolts (hopefully into one of your nets), be ready to sprint to the hole and despatch it with a well aimed blow from your priest. While doing this, cover the hole with your foot to prevent the next rabbit from making good his escape. I like to carry a few spare purse nets in my pocket to put over the holes while I free the dead rabbit from the net – a job which can sometimes take quite a few minutes.

It is important to empty the rabbit's bladder as soon as possible after its death, otherwise the

The net bag can be used to stop a hole if you run out of purse nets.

Lift up the corner of the purse net and allow the ferret to walk down the hole at her own speed.

Be alert to ferrets leaving the burrow.

urine will taint the meat. To do this, simply hold the rabbit with its back against your leg and run your fingers down its stomach, starting just below the rib cage and finishing at the vent. It is usually at this time that the next rabbit hits one of your other nets!

By listening carefully, often with your head well into the mouth of a hole, it is sometimes possible to tell exactly where the ferrets are and what they are doing. By using an electronic detector, it is simplicity itself to keep tabs on the workers. The detector is held vertically (as indicated in the manufacturer's instructions) and swept across the area until the signal is heard. With practice, it is possible to pinpoint the ferret to within fifteen to twenty centimetres (six to eight inches).

If the ferret does not move for a few minutes, this may indicate that she has made a kill, or that a rabbit has run into a stop (a tunnel with a dead end) and that she is trying to move it. There is little that you can do, other than dig down to her; this should only be done as a last resort and never before you have finished working the burrow. Mark the spot for later investigation.

When good working ferrets fail to find the rabbits in a particular tunnel, they will often return to the surface and, in some cases, make their own way to another opening. You should always be aware enough to notice the emergence of a ferret; at that time, you can carry her to the tunnel of your choice and introduce her. Experienced ferrets will be able to pass through purse nets without disturbing them, but it always pays to check.

When it is obvious that all of the rabbits are out of the burrow, call up your ferrets and box them. This is easily done if they have become accustomed to a specific sound at their normal feeding time. I always make a point of rattling a bunch of keys at such times and, when this is repeated in the field, it almost always has the desired effect, i.e. it brings the ferrets out where I can reach them.

Some ferrets develop the extremely annoying habit of staying inside the tunnel, just out of reach; this is known as 'skulking' and is usually caused by impatient handlers grabbing at their ferrets before they have totally emerged from the hole. Always wait until your ferret is well clear of the hole before,

Listening, with an ear to the ground, can help to ascertain the state of play underground.

68

*Experienced ferrets will be able to pass through
purse nets without disturbing them.*

*Enticing a skulking ferret to leave a burrow,
using a dead rabbit.*

slowly, reaching to pick her up. If your ferrets
develop the habit, it can be cured, but it takes
time. To encourage a skulking ferret to exit a
dig, dangle a paunched rabbit just inside the
hole, luring the ferret into the open with it.
Once the ferret is well clear of the hole, gently
and slowly pick it up, making encouraging
noises to her.

Very occasionally, even the most well be-
haved ferret may decide to lay-up and no
amount of coaxing will dislodge the errant
animal. If digging is either impossible or you
are just not able to locate the ferret, then it
may be necessary to leave the ferret underground overnight. This should only be a last
measure and never become common practice.

Go around the area and carefully and thoroughly block every exit/entrance to the
burrow except one. Near to this open hole,
place a couple of cage-type traps. These are
available commercially (known as 'live catch'
traps), or it is possible to build one yourself.
These should be baited – usually with rabbit
entrails – and then placed as near to the hole
as possible, the idea being that the ferret
will eventually emerge from the dig and be

A 'live catch' trap.

A recaptured ferret.

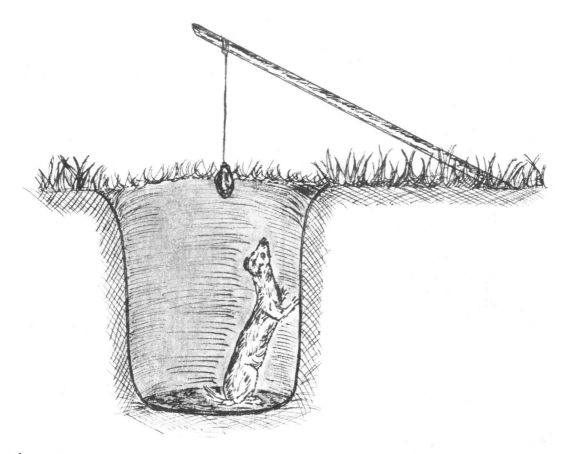

A ferret catch pit.

attracted to the smell of the meat. Once she has entered the cage and tripped the trap, she will be safe until you arrive early the next morning to take her home.

Murphy's Law being what it is, there will come a time when a ferret lays up and you do not have a cage trap with you; do not despair! Carry out the exit blocking routine described above and then dig a couple of deep pits (about seventy-five centimetres (thirty inches) deep and at least seventy-five centimetres (thirty inches) wide), with sheer sides close to the open exit. Tie a lump of rabbit flesh or entrails to the end of a piece of string approximately twenty-five centimetres (ten inches) long, attached to a piece of wood (a small, strong branch will be ideal) which is long enough to wedge across the top of the pit, and suspend the

meat from it into the centre of the hole. Bait and prepare both pits in this way. The idea is to entice the ferret to try to grab the meat, at which time she will fall into the pit, from where she cannot escape. Whichever method you employ to catch your errant *mustelid*, it is vital that you return regularly to check the traps, otherwise your ferret – and possibly other animals – could suffer unduly.

If you think that a rabbit has been killed underground, now is the time to check it out by digging in the suspected areas. A good indicator of a ferret/rabbit encounter is the presence of rabbit fur in the ferret's claws.

If your morning has been very busy, you will not have had time to paunch the rabbits and, indeed, some ferreters prefer to do this at home. However, in warm weather this

Paunching a rabbit in the field.

operation must be carried out as soon after the rabbits' death as possible, or the meat will be tainted and thus inedible. (Full details of this operation are given in Chapter 14.) At this stage, I like to give my ferrets a drink of milk and a snack – usually of rabbit liver, kidneys and heart.

When all of your ferrets are safely in their carrying box, you can begin to gather in the purse nets. Remember to count them all as you are collecting and folding them. As a safety precaution, count them again before placing them in your carrying bag. Carrying all of the equipment, ferrets and the dead rabbits can often be quite a task. If a large number of rabbits have been killed, it may be easier to 'leg' them and carry them on the spade handle, over one shoulder. To 'leg' or 'hock' a rabbit, cut one of the tendons on the back leg and pass the other hind leg through it. Then, simply pass the haft of the spade through the gap between the hind legs.

On arrival back at home, make sure that the ferrets are settled back into their cub before going on to other things; after all, without their assistance and hard work, you would not have had much sport. Check their bodies for cuts and grazes and remove any thorns. Pay special attention to their feet, removing any mud. Give them a good meal and then leave them alone to rest, while you clean your kit and prepare the rabbits for the freezer, or even immediate eating, before taking a well earned (and much needed), bath. Remember to hang your purse nets where they can dry thoroughly.

8

Equipment

'Judge not a man by his clothes.'
Thomas Dewar

It is always a tendency, in any hobby or sport, for the beginner to amass large quantities of equipment and gadgets, many of which are of no use at all and are, therefore, a complete waste of money. Do not think that any equipment – no matter how fancy or sophisticated – will compensate for inadequacies in your own knowledge and/or experience. Experience cannot be bought – only amassed.

The following list gives details of some of the equipment that I now use, have tried, or feel strongly about. It does not seek to be the definitive list of recommended or essential equipment. Every experienced ferreter has his or her own ideas on this (and every other ferret) subject.

Equipment List

Ferrets The number required will be determined by the area to be worked and by the number available to the ferreter. I prefer to work jills and would never attempt any bury

The equipment bag, complete with nets, detectors, lines and priest.

with less than two. If a liner is to be used, this figure would obviously be three. In large warrens, I like to take along at least two pairs of free working jills and a liner. The two 'teams' are worked either all together (in a very large warren), or interchanged during the day.

Since the introduction of electronic detectors, I no longer use a liner in the traditional way, if at all. If I have a 'lay-up', I use a hob as above but, instead of fitting him with a line, which all too frequently snags on underground roots and other such obstacles, I fit him with an electronic transmitter attached to his collar. He does exactly the same job, i.e. he finds the errant free working jill and/or the dead rabbit and, after having chased off the jill, he curls up at the side of the kill to await my digging him out. With practice, this method can save many hours of hard digging.

Carry Box The ferrets must, of course, be transported to and from the working area and, to my mind, they deserve to travel in comfort.

I do not like carrying bags or sacks as they give the inmates very little protection from the cold, the wet or size nine feet! A good carrying box (measuring about 45 × 25 × 25cm (18 × 10 × 10in)) is a far better method of transporting the ferrets. The carry boxes must be of stout construction, while remaining reasonably light. They must be weatherproof, but would benefit from a couple of small drainage holes in the bottom, for obvious reasons.

I find it beneficial to have two completely separate compartments, enabling me to select which ferrets to use, but ensuring that the others do not escape while my attention is elsewhere. Adequate ventilation holes must be provided in each compartment. Before venturing out on the hunting foray, provide the ferrets with an ample quantity of wood shavings and hay, to absorb moisture, to keep them warm and also to prevent them from being knocked around too much during transport. The box should have a strong, broad carrying

A sturdy carrying box will protect ferrets against the weather and clumsy feet.

It is a good idea to have two separate compartments. Adequate ventilation must be provided in each compartment.

strap, secured to the box at the correct length to ensure reasonable comfort for you whilst carrying the box.

Electronic Detector   I first started to use an electronic ferret detector about ten years ago and have never looked back. Used correctly and with care, they save much digging and help ensure that no dead rabbits are left underground and, therefore, wasted.

The detector consists of a pre-tuned receiver and a collar-mounted transmitter. The early models were rather large but, using modern technological developments, they are now produced in quite tiny forms. Although quite expensive, they do last for many years, if looked after and properly maintained. Only one receiver is required, but each ferret should be equipped with her own collar.

Before entering a ferret wearing such a collar, wrap a piece of plastic insulating tape around both the transmitter, to secure the fastening, and the loose end of the collar, to help minimise the risks of it becoming snagged and/or the collar coming adrift during the ferret's underground excursions.

Some ferreters prefer to use their free working ferrets without transmitters and, instead, utilise a hob fitted with one. This hob is used in exactly the same way as a liner, except without the line being attached to his collar. He is only introduced when you have reason to believe that there has been an underground kill and/or one of your free workers has laid up. I like to use all of my ferrets with radio transmitter collars attached, so that I can keep in touch with all of the subterranean happenings.

In use, the receiver must be held upright (as indicated on the side of most makes) and swung about thirty centimetres (one foot) above the ground where the ferret is thought to be. Once your detector picks up the signal from the ferret's collar transmitter, the receiver will start to make a noise; this is usually, depending on the make, a loud and rapid 'ticking' noise. When this noise is heard, move more carefully until you have narrowed the area down to about one metre (three feet) square. By adjusting the control on the receiver, you will reduce the sensitivity of the detector and so, by carefully moving the receiver and reducing its sensitivity, it is possible to track a ferret while she is working underground and, when she stops, to find her position to within about five to ten centimetres (two to four inches). Practice makes perfect!

After use, the batteries should be removed from the transmitter and the collars and their attachments thoroughly cleaned and dried, prior to storage. Never store the transmitters or receivers with their batteries still in place. Leakage can occur and cause damage; this will be expensive (and often impossible) to rectify.

A hob ferret fitted with an electronic detector.

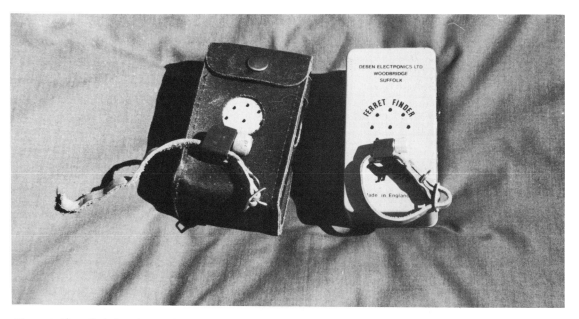

Electronic 'ferret finder' receivers.

Insulation Tape Good quality, plastic insulation tape has many uses on a ferreting day, including those outlined above, and a roll should always be carried. The terminals of spare batteries can be protected against short circuits by a piece of this material, and loose ends of collars, belts and straps secured to prevent them from snagging.

Spade Although I always hope that I will not need to dig, I always take the precaution of including a suitable spade in my equipment. The traditional tool for digging out is called a 'chad' or a 'graft', but any small-bladed spade of strong, top quality construction will do the job.

Whichever design or make you go for, ensure that it is strong enough for the job. All good quality tools are expensive and skimping on these is courting disaster. After use, clean the whole instrument and wipe an oily rag over the blade. This will ensure that your investment enjoys a long and useful life.

A spade or 'graft'.

Mink Trap This is an important piece of ferreting equipment which should always be taken along on any ferreting trip – even if it is then left in the car and not needed. Should one (or more) of your ferrets be lost underground and you need to leave the area, setting one of these live catch traps will help you to recapture the errant *mustelid* during the night, while you are fast asleep in your bed. (Full details of its use are contained in Chapter 7).

Milk During a day's work, the ferrets will become tired and thirsty and they deserve to be given a little light refreshment. By including a small container of milk and a small dish in your equipment, the ferrets can enjoy a 'tea break' while you have yours.

Purse Nets These are nets which are placed over the entrance/exit holes to the bury, into which (hopefully) the rabbits will bolt. As their name suggests, they are designed on the same principle as the old-fashioned drawstring purses.

No matter how many are taken on a hunting trip, I never seem to have enough. The minimum that I would recommend for any ferreter to carry is twenty. This is usually sufficient for most buries. They come in an assortment of sizes, colours, materials and qualities.

To my mind, colour does not matter, as rabbits are said to be colour-blind and, in any case, as they are fleeing from their pursuer, they are hardly likely to balk at a blue net but run into a green one! I have used nets dyed red, blue, yellow, green, brown, black and many other colours – all with varying degrees of success. The most important aspect of purse nets is their setting – get that wrong, and no net, regardless of colour, will rectify your mistakes.

Traditionally, all nets were made from hemp or other such natural substances and, today, many ferreters still prefer to use these materials. Personally, I find advantages and disadvantages with both natural and manmade materials. Hemp rots if stored while still

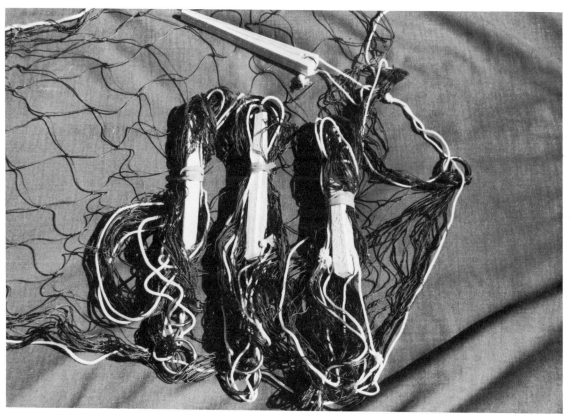

Purse nets.

damp; nylon does not. Nylon slips very easily, making it unsuitable for some applications. Hemp nets are relatively expensive when compared to those made from nylon. I prefer to use an assortment of materials, predominantly nylon, but with a few hemp nets for awkward sites.

All purse nets must be well made, utilising two good quality rings. The material – whether hemp or nylon – must also be top quality and the mesh should be big enough to allow an adult ferret to pass through easily, but not a rabbit. A knot to knot size of about five to six centimetres (two to three inches) is generally accepted as the correct size of mesh.

Around the neck of the purse net is the draw-string, which actually purses the net when a rabbit hits it. This draw-string must be made of strong material and the ends securely tied to a peg. It is not unknown for rabbits to escape from purse nets when a badly tied knot

comes adrift. If using nylon for the draw-strings, utilise a double fisherman's knot.

The pegs that hold the net into the ground are usually made from well-seasoned hazel, sharpened at one end and a hole drilled through the other (through which the draw-string is fastened). However, there are times when the ground is just too hard for these pegs to be driven in. At such times, I prefer to use metal pegs, such as meat skewers or tent pegs.

During transit, all nets must be folded in such a way that they are easy to deploy and, after use, they should be cleaned thoroughly and allowed to dry before being put into storage. This is particularly true in the case of hemp nets.

Purse nets (and long nets) can be home-made, providing that one has the time, patience and skill, thus saving money (home-made nets can work out at about a quarter of the cost of bought nets). I have tried this, with

Double fisherman's knot.

limited success, but I do not have a lot of spare time, preferring to use what little I have to actually go ferreting. It is worthwhile giving net-making a try though – who knows, you may even get to like it!

Long Nets Long nets are used instead of, or sometimes to supplement the use of, purse nets. Made from either hemp or nylon, they are deployed around a large bury or across the bottom of a bank, where they should, if correctly set, catch any rabbits which manage to successfully bolt away from the hole. The standard length for a modern long net is one hundred metres (a hundred and ten yards). They can also be bought in twenty-five and fifty metre lengths (twenty-seven and fifty-five yards). Several nets are often joined together to produce netting for a particular use. Again, long nets can be home-made, in which case any length at all can be produced.

Stakes are required to support long nets. As with the pegs for the purse net, the preferred material is well-seasoned hazel. Ensure that they are given a good point, to ease their fixing in the ground, which is often rock hard.

A purse net folded for transporting.

Cord Both purse nets and long nets depend upon the use of good quality cord and so an extra supply is a useful addition to a ferreter's outfit. Again, either hemp or nylon can be used; I favour nylon.

Knife Two knives – a sheath and a lock-knife – should always be carried on a hunting trip. The sheath knife is used for hacking away foliage or cutting branches to use as probes. The lock-knife is used for gutting the rabbits. Ensure that both knives are kept sharp, as a blunt blade is worse than useless.

Knee Pads During a day's ferreting, much time is spent on hands and knees, often resulting in painful swollen and/or bruised joints. To help prevent this and alleviate the discomfort of kneeling on rough ground for long periods, a pair of padded, leather knee-pads are worth their weight in gold. These can be purchased from specialist ferret equipment shops and also from garden suppliers. It is often possible to purchase these pads from miners, since they too spend a lot of time on their knees and most colliery workers will possess a pair or two of knee pads.

Priest A priest is a type of cosh, designed for killing rabbits humanely. In order to make it more effective, the top end of the priest is often weighted with lead, or some other heavy material. Two other methods may be used to despatch the animals – the classic 'rabbit punch' or pulling the rabbit's neck. I have tried all three methods and favour the priest as the most humane method. A sharp blow to the back of the head is all that is required.

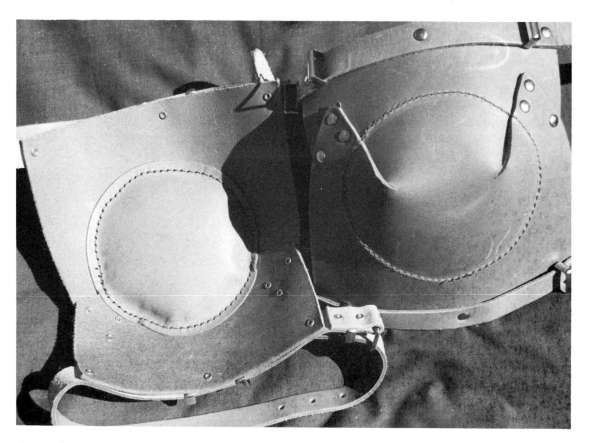

Knee pads.

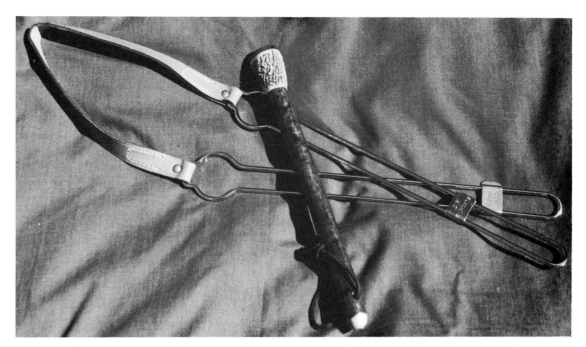

A priest and a game carrier

Probe Traditionally, this is a blunt-ended, metal (usually iron) rod with a small bulge about ten centimetres (four inches) from the point. It is used to trace the path of a tunnel by pushing it into the ground and feeling for lack of resistance. This must be done very carefully as, even though it has a blunt point, it can still injure the ferret if used too harshly. The bulge in the rod makes an oversize hole. If one takes the time and trouble to make or buy one of these instruments, care should be taken to ensure that it is not left behind or buried while out in the field. Painting it with fluorescent paint, or attaching a brightly coloured cloth to the top end, will help to ensure its longevity.

Collars and Line If liners are used in the traditional way, then their collars should be made of best quality, soft leather; the material can be kept supple by the use of saddle soap or 'Mars Oil'. The line should be of nylon and at least ten metres (ten yards) long and attached to the collar via a good quality swivel. Marking the line with a waterproof ink mark every

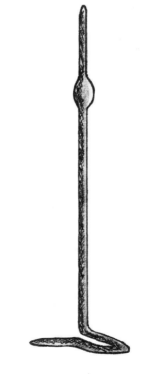

A probe.

81

metre (yard) will help to gauge how far the liner has travelled underground. Never mark the line by tying knots in it; these invariably cause many problems by constantly snagging on every underground obstacle that the hob comes to.

Bells   Some ferreters insist on fastening a bell to a collar on every one of their working ferrets in the belief that this will enable them to keep a better control over their charges. I do not hold with this school of thought, finding such items irritating and of no practical benefit.

Secateurs   A pair of good quality secateurs will prove beneficial, especially when it is necessary to clear the area of brambles and other such growths. Either attach them to your belt or some other piece of equipment, or get into the habit of always pocketing them after use, as otherwise they will soon be lost. Painting the handles with fluorescent paint will also help.

Muzzles and Copes   I do not hold with the use of either muzzles or copes. For a working ferret to be disabled in this way is very dangerous (for the ferret) as, if it should meet a rat while working, it cannot possibly defend itself. Likewise, if a muzzled ferret were to escape, it would be sentenced to a long, lingering death by starvation. Many people who advocate the use of such devices do so because they cannot – or will not – take the time and trouble to tame their ferret and get it used to being handled. At one time, such people would have their ferrets' teeth extracted or even sew their lips together – illegal and cruel practices which have, hopefully, been relegated to history.

Many vets, however, refuse to handle ferrets unless they are muzzled to remove any danger of being bitten. In such cases, a muzzle made from soft, supple leather is recommended. These can be purchased from many country sports shops. Accustom your ferrets to wearing them before they are needed.

A ferret cope.

Clothing

Although it is true to say that almost any old clothing is suitable for ferreting, there are certain criteria which this clothing must meet. It is obvious that all outer garments must be windproof and, preferably, waterproof. They should also be roomy enough to allow free movement, without causing discomfort. The items listed below will provide a guide and a base on which the individual can build.

Hat   A hat is essential wear. It will help maintain the body's temperature (about twenty per cent of body heat can be lost from an uncovered head), and protect against thorns and other such items. Wool is warm and, to a certain degree, weatherproof but has an annoying habit of collecting all kinds of debris. I favour either a flat cap or a 'bush hat', preferably of thorn-proof material.

Jacket   The wax-proof jacket has gained almost universal support from the country sports enthusiast but is not ideal for ferreting. I prefer to employ an ex-army combat jacket, taking a wax-proof only for wear in the rain.

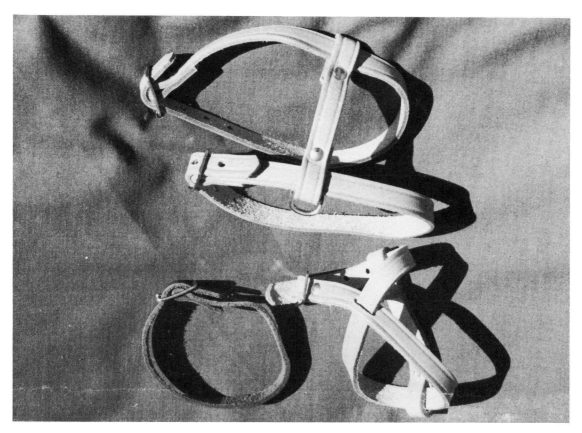

Harness, collar and muzzle suitable for ferrets (though not while working).

Trousers Again, ex-army clothing is ideal; it is possible to buy windproof trousers from government surplus shops. A pair of wax-proof leggings are ideal for extra protection against thorns and the wet.

Underclothes As temperatures have a habit of remaining low during ferreting operations, thermal underclothes are essential. There are many different styles to choose from; I personally favour long-sleeved silk vests and matching 'long-johns'.

Socks When your feet are cold, you are cold. I always wear two pairs of medium length socks made from pure wool. 'Loop-stitch' socks are more comfortable and warmer than ordinary ones. In very cold weather, I supplement these with a pair of

thermal inner socks, which are extremely thin but remarkably effective.

Boots During deep snow or very wet conditions, I wear a pair of rubber wellingtons. These do not, however, give much protection against the cold and so, normally, I will wear a pair of high-leg leather boots. This footwear should be large enough to allow for the wearing of extra socks.

Spares Clothes worn during a ferreting expedition have a nasty habit of becoming very wet, dirty and smelly! For this reason, it is advisable to have a complete change of clothing and footwear in the car to change into, along with a couple of towels for drying yourself with. A large plastic bag will be useful to place the dirty clothing in.

9

Dogs and Guns

'A ferret may be put into the burrows and the rabbits shot as they bolt out; but this is so rapid a motion that great quickness of shot will be necessary.'

Anonymous

There are occasions when you may not want to use your ferrets in conjunction with purse nets, but will instead utilise either dogs, guns or a combination of the two. This can often be more 'sporting' than using nets, but it will not give you such a high return of rabbits. The use of dogs and/or guns also requires more planning and the training to a very high degree of competence and obedience of both the dogs and the Guns (i.e. those who will be shooting).

There are several types of dogs which can be used for the job of ferreting, all of which have specific roles to play. These are terriers, gaze hounds (i.e. those dogs which hunt by sight, rather than the smell of their quarry), retrievers (for the retrieval of shot rabbits) and hunting dogs such as spaniels.

Terriers

The word 'terrier' derives from the Latin *terra*, meaning earth or ground and from this one can ascertain that they were originally bred to work underground. They are, in fact, still used for that purpose.

There are many different breeds of terriers, all of which have their adherents. These breeds include the Lakeland, Border, Fox and Jack Russell terriers. I personally prefer the Jack Russell and would always choose this breed – providing that it had come from a good working background. This is important to remember because, unless you are very lucky, Jack Russells bred for the pet trade do not usually come up to scratch when it comes to marking and hunting rabbits.

After having said that, I must point out that I once acquired a Jack Russell which came from an unknown pedigree and which proved to be one of the best working terriers that I have come across. At the time, I was working on a local radio station in Sheffield, where I had a programme about animals – their keeping, habits, health, etc. – and, at the end of one of these programmes, I received a phone call from a lady who had been given a tiny Jack Russell bitch puppy by a girl who had acquired her but could not keep her. The lady asked if I could, perhaps through my programme, find the puppy a good home. Before I knew it, I was driving to a village just outside Barnsley to see the pup (I think that I just wanted an excuse to acquire yet another dog!)

The Jack Russell was so tiny that she fitted comfortably in the palm of my hand, and I estimated that she was only about four or five weeks old – too young for her to be away from her mother. I could not resist her, in fact, I did not even try, and was soon on the way home, complete with a tiny, contented puppy curled up in my lap.

At home, I introduced Brit (I had christened her within five minutes of seeing her) to my English Springer Spaniel bitch and her six-week-old puppy and soon the three of them were happily sharing their kennel and everything else, as if they were all the same family. In fact, as the Springer was still feeding her own puppy, it was not long before Brit found the milk supply and she, too, was being suckled! I am sure that, without the maternal care and feeding lavished upon her by the Springer, Brit would have had a very difficult

A Jack Russell Terrier.

time and would not have grown up as well as she did.

During her early, formative weeks, I made sure that she was introduced to the ferrets – a very important part of the education of any dog that is to be expected to work with them. At first, Brit wanted to chase and grab them but, with perseverance and firmness on my part and much good nature on the ferrets' part, Brit finally realised that they were neither toys nor potential food.

When autumn came around and I went off to catch a few rabbits for the table (and to feed my horde of ferrets), it seemed natural that I should take Brit along with me. I still remember the first time that, during a training session, she found a used rabbit hole; she sniffed around the area and at the entrance to every hole that she could find until, after having sniffed at one particular tunnel entrance, she ran back to me at full speed and leapt up in front of me. Having thus gained my attention, she then ran back to the hole and stood, stock still, at the entrance, her undocked tail wagging furiously.

Unwilling to trust her too much at this crucial stage, I put her on her lead and secured her to a nearby tree before opening my carry box and putting a couple of loose ferrets down the tunnel that she had found, and another close by. As the second ferret disappeared down the hole, a flash of brown fur rocketed from a hole that I had failed to notice. Luckily (as it turned out), I had also failed to tie Brit too securely and, with a tug on her lead, she came free and ran at the escaping rabbit, which she caught easily and despatched with a couple of quick shakes.

This was to be Brit's hallmark – the quiet scenting out of burrows with rabbits at home and the purposeful run, catch and quick despatch of her quarry, whether it be rabbit or rat. Unlike many terriers, she did not bark while waiting, often very long times, for the quarry to bolt and neither did she scratch or dig at the burrows that she found. Although to this day I have never found out where she actually came from, I know that she must have come from a long line of working Jack Russells with instincts such as hers!

Although there are no guaranteed ways of ensuring that you will end up with a good worker, there are a few guidelines which will help to put the odds in your favour when choosing a terrier for rabbiting.

As stated earlier, it is best if you choose a pup from a good working line. If possible, try to see the parents working but always try to see at least one of the parents and pay careful attention to the conditions that the dogs are kept in. Also, try to ascertain the nature of the parents since, although Jack Russells should always be tough and never give quarter to their adversaries, they also need to be handleable and easy for both you and your family to get on with. Look for cuts and sores on the pup, especially on its belly and check for signs of diarrhoea. Avoid any animal that appears sick, injured or is aggressive. I always choose the pup which is curious and, while not rushing at you, is easily encouraged to investigate your hands.

Colour, size and markings are all personal choices and have no bearing whatsoever on the working (or any other) qualities of any animal.

Gaze Hounds

This class includes whippets and greyhounds as well as the cross-breeds commonly referred to as 'lurchers'. They range in size from the diminutive whippets to the massive deer hound types; again, all have their own champions. This type of dog is used to chase the rabbit (and other quarry), to catch it, kill it and return it to the dog's master or mistress. It should, however, be noted that all of these dogs require to be able to see their quarry and, in thick cover, they may not be able to do so. They are best used, therefore, in open country and, to my mind, are not as useful to the average ferreter as a good terrier.

A 'lurcher'.

Retrievers

If bolting rabbits are to be shot, retrievers such as the Labrador, Golden or Flat-Coated, are useful to fetch the dead animals but, other than this, they are of little or no use to ferreters, since a good retriever is trained not to chase, nor to pick up and kill live rabbits or other animals.

Spaniels

Although it could be argued that spaniels are of no use to ferreters for the same reasons that make retrievers unsuitable, they do have at least one use which the thinking ferreter might take advantage of. By allowing a well-trained Springer to hunt the hedges and bushes around the working area before ferreting begins, outlying rabbits will be encouraged to seek shelter in their underground homes. However, the importance of only using a well-trained spaniel cannot be over emphasised. The idea is to merely worry the rabbits, causing them to return underground, rather than terrifying them to such an extent that they will run to ground for their very lives, as this will make them much more liable to stay underground and face the ferrets (with all of the risk of lay-ups and underground kills), than rush out and face a killer dog!

Guns

Shooting bolting rabbits is one of the most exciting country sports that I have ever participated in. It involves the use of ferrets, guns, dogs and one's friends. It can, however, also end friendships if the day is not properly regulated.

The best type of area to use for this sport is where a burrow is in a slight hillock, with plenty of open (or at least semi-open) space around it. This enables the Guns to stand on the top of the hill when the ferrets have been introduced underground and to shoot at the bolting rabbits without taking unsafe shots which might endanger other Guns. Usually, however, the type of land available is not ideal and, in these cases, even more care than usual must be employed by all participants on the day. The safety of all who take part in country sports is paramount at all times.

The almost universally accepted caliber of shotgun for shooting rabbits in this way is the 12-bore. The cartridges recommended are No. 6 size. The Guns must be placed at appropriate points around the area and each given specific areas where they can shoot, just as in formal driven shooting. It is also important to tell each Gun where all the other Guns are standing, so that no one takes a seemingly safe shot where a man may be standing completely out of sight.

Participants must also be instructed not to shoot at any rabbit until it is seen and positively identified. This will usually mean that the rabbit is well clear of any cover and it must always be well clear of the tunnel entrance, since a wounded rabbit may well drag itself back underground, where it will die a long, lingering death and result in waste. They are also, sometimes, not rabbits! It is often some time after the introduction of the ferrets that rabbits begin to bolt and occasionally, shooters get rather impatient. This causes them to take shots at times (and targets) that they would otherwise not.

I remember taking a few friends along on a shooting foray with my ferrets. I placed all of the Guns at their stands and gave them strict instructions about where and at what to shoot. I then entered my ferrets and took up my own shooting position. After about five minutes, the rabbits began to bolt, all from one side of the dig. About a dozen rabbits fell to the Guns within almost as many minutes and then no more appeared for some time. One of the Guns, who had been on the side away from all of the action and had not fired a shot or even seen a rabbit must have been getting rather bored and this boredom soon turned to impatience. When he heard a noise to his front and then glimpsed a piece of brownish fur, he shot blindly into the gorse.

His shot was true, and the animal died immediately. Unfortunately, the dead animal was not a rabbit – it was one of my ferrets. When his retriever brought the limp and lifeless body back to him and he realised his tragic mistake, he called me over. 'Sorry', he said, 'but it's only a ferret. Here's a pound to buy another one. Let's get on with the shooting.' I cannot write here the words that I used, but suffice it to say that I left him in no doubt as to my feelings, nor as to the place where he could put his pound note! My ferrets are just as important to me as are my spaniels and terriers and I was not going to risk their (and perhaps my own) life by allowing the sport to continue. I called a halt to the whole proceedings and told the errant shot never to expect another invitation from me.

I give this narrative merely to illustrate how carefully one must choose one's hunting companions and how stringently all rules and safety measures must be adhered to at all times. If you have colleagues whose shooting and behaviour you can trust, then shooting bolting rabbits over ferrets is a sport second to none. It does not produce the quantity of rabbits that netting does, but it does make up for it in other ways.

When I take people with me on such a hunt, I prefer not to use a gun myself, but to concentrate on the ferrets, retrieval and despatch of any wounded rabbits and I would commend this approach to all who wish to try this exciting aspect of the sport. If, however, you are limited in the number of Guns that you can call upon, then you will have little choice and will have to use a gun yourself.

The secret of a successful outing, as with all things, is to take care and not rush. Keep quiet when not actually shooting and move about as little as possible. Before leaving the area at the end of the day, it is always worth working a spaniel through the undergrowth around the area, just in case a rabbit or two has been missed.

10

Ratting with Ferrets

'For the rat collectively, I have not a good word to say.'
Frances Pitt

Although most ferreters will only ever hunt the European rabbit, the rat can also provide excellent sport, which in turn helps to control this pest. Again, it is necessary that would-be hunters know something about the natural history of their quarry.

Types of Rats

Legend has it that, prior to the Crusades, Britain was devoid of any rats. It is said that the black rat (*Rattus rattus*) originated in the Far East and came to Britain on board returning troop ships. By the thirteenth century, the black rat (and also the plague, or 'Black Death') was firmly established in Britain. It is a commonly held belief that the black rat was totally responsible for the 'Black Death', but this is only partially true. The black rat did indeed carry the plague germ (*Pasteurella pestis*) in its blood, but it was fleas which spread the disease from the rats to humans. At that time in our history, not only rats but also every human had fleas. Part of the life cycle of the flea involves them laying their eggs in a dusty (some would say dirty) place, such as the floor of a human home. This obviously necessitated their leaving the host animal (in this case a rat). This task complete, the flea would hop on to the first animal it found (including humans), sink in its jaws and feed on the blood. This is how the plague spread.

The brown rat is said to have come to these shores on board ships from Norway, as its scientific name, *Rattus norwegicus* records. This has never been totally proven; some authorities believe that it came from China, while others think that it originated from around the Caspian Sea. Wherever it came from, the brown rat was about to invade, colonise and generally take over Britain.

Arriving in the 1720s, *Rattus norwegicus* soon replaced the black rat; there are many reasons for this. Unlike the black rat, which needed the warmth and shelter of human homes, the brown rat was equally at home in burrows, corn ricks, stables, barns, poultry houses and even in the damp coldness of the new sewers which were, by now, in place in most big towns and cities. The brown rat was much bigger than its black cousin and, although this meant that the black was more agile than the brown rat, the brown's extra size enabled it to secure a place on ground level (the black rat preferred to live off the ground, reflecting its tree living ancestors).

Some authorities credit the brown rat with the extermination of the black rat, as the brown often killed and fed on the black. Not only did *Rattus norwegicus* feed on some of its black cousins, it also ate its food supplies. *Rattus rattus* was doomed and crept away, almost into extinction. Nowadays, he is only to be found in isolated pockets, such as a few small villages in the east of England, and also in the upper floors of some of the warehouses of the London dock area.

Anyone hunting rats today will, therefore, be almost certainly hunting *Rattus norwegicus*. Do not let the common name mislead you – *Rattus norwegicus* comes in many colours. The pet or 'fancy' rat is, in fact, the brown rat, though it is often any colour but brown.

This rat is to be found in almost every place that the human race has ever occupied. There

Rattus norwegicus, *the brown rat.*

are even reports that it will soon have colonised parts of Antarctica. It can feed on almost any type of food that humans can – and on many that we cannot. It is not easy to control by poison, as it will always be extremely wary of any new substance, eating very little at a time. The species also has the ability to pass on information about risky food sources and substances (probably through its faeces). It is aggressive, not tolerating any other animal (or bird) in its vicinity. It is also a savage fighter; a doe rat protecting her litter is a match for almost any other creature of comparative (and often greater) size. In short, it is a formidable foe.

In Britain, the brown rat tends to live in sewers (which will not interest any but the most ardent rat chaser), on rubbish tips, in barns and in poultry houses (usually under the floor boards).

Hunting the Brown Rat

There are several different methods of hunting the brown rat but, before considering these, it must be pointed out that hunting rats is not without its dangers. Wild rats can – and usually do – carry many diseases. One of the most common is Weil's Disease, or leptospirosis (sometimes called leptospiral jaundice and commonly known as 'Rat Catcher's Yellows'). This is caused by spirochaetes, a type of bacteria. In common with other bacteria, it causes a fever once it has entered the blood stream (perhaps through a cut or graze on the hand), produces toxic substances and can sometimes kill.

For some reason, as yet unknown, these bacteria do not affect the host animal, the rat, which is therefore known as a passive carrier. It is thought that the rat and the spirochaetes may have evolved together, since the bacteria require a host animal in which they can survive and which they do not damage, in order that the bacteria themselves are not wiped out.

Some of the bacteria are passed out in the rat's urine and if a human gets some of that urine on a cut or graze, he is infected. Likewise, eating food with hands which are soiled with rat urine (for example, after a successful foray against *Rattus norwegicus*) is a sure way of infecting one's body. The first symptoms appear within a few days of infection. Fevers, diarrhoea, severe thigh pains and vomiting are some of these symptoms. Within a week, the victim is jaundiced, owing to liver damage. It is usually at this stage that the family doctor is given some indication of the nature of the illness and, if he is to treat the patient successfully, he must move quickly, since if he does not, and the patient's own immune system is not too strong, the patient may be dead within the next seven to ten days.

This information is not intended to frighten the reader, merely to inform him or her of the possible dangers of hunting the rat. The danger can be minimised by the wearing of strong rubber gloves at all times when hunting rats and also by adhering to a strict hygiene routine, i.e. always washing hands well before eating or drinking.

A few years ago, I was awakened in the middle of the night by searing pains and chronic diarrhoea. A few days later I looked at my reflection in the mirror and I saw a bright yellow face staring back at me. I realised that this was jaundice, and made arrangements to see my local doctor. He took blood samples and sent them off for analysis, ordering me to rest until I returned for the results a few days later. The results were positive and the doctor informed me that I had a mild case of hepatitis. There was no real treatment, he told me – only rest. I returned home and tried to do just that.

It was during this time that, being totally bored, I sent a friend to the library to fetch some books which might help to while away the time. Knowing my interest in country sports and particularly in ferrets, my friend brought a selection of appropriate books back for me. One of them was by Brian Plummer and gave instructions on ferreting rabbits and rats, along with more than a few interesting stories. The bit that I found interesting, however, almost scared me to death.

Mr Plummer described, in graphic detail, an illness where all of the symptoms matched mine. He did not, however, refer to the disease as hepatitis, but as leptospirosis – Weil's Disease. I have never had my own diagnosis confirmed, my doctor merely said that it was a possibility but, as I had been hunting rats a few days before the onset of my illness, I have no doubt that I had had a mild attack of Weil's Disease. It took many months before I was fighting fit again and, so concerned did I become by the thought that the disease could have killed me, that I have never hunted rats with my ferrets since.

If, despite this dire warning, you are still intent on hunting the rat with your ferrets, there are precautions that you should take if you are to avoid the risk of contracting one of the many diseases that wild rats can carry. As stated earlier, strong, well-fitting rubber gloves should be worn at all times. The heavy duty rubber gloves sold in hardware stores are ideal. If they are too bulky, or do not fit well, they will quickly become a nuisance and you will stop wearing them.

The ferrets and dogs that you use for your rat hunting must also be protected, although protective garments for them are hardly practical. It is, however, possible (and advisable) to have all of your animals vaccinated against leptospirosis and other rat-borne diseases. After all, prevention is better than cure. Even so, it is still often necessary to carry out first aid treatment on some of your animals.

After every hunting trip (while you are still wearing your rubber gloves), ferrets and dogs must be closely examined for any cuts or abrasions. These must be thoroughly cleaned with a good antiseptic. To do this, it will be necessary for some of the animal's fur to be clipped off. After washing well, dry by dabbing with a piece of cotton wool and then apply some wound dusting powder (available from your local veterinary surgeon). It is always best to take any seriously injured animal to the vet at the earliest possible opportunity. The vet will decide if any antibiotics are required.

Both dogs and ferrets should be given a good bath a short time after any excursions against rats. Not only will this help to reduce the risk of infection from any rat urine which is on the coat of the animal, it will also help you to notice any cuts or abrasions which may otherwise go unnoticed.

Choice of Ferrets

Ferrets which are to be used for ratting must be special. They should be small enough to work their way through holes and tunnels that the rats will use, and yet still be strong enough to fight (and hopefully defeat) the rats that they meet. Like all ferrets, they must be completely trustworthy as, after a fight with a rat, even the most docile ferret is likely to be so angry and excited that she may well give a good nip to any hand that is pushed towards her in the wrong manner. As always, gentle, soft-talking and slow deliberate movements are the way to sooth an excited animal. Take your time. Five minutes spent reassuring your ferrets (or dogs) after a bit of a scrap, will be time well spent.

Ferrets should never be knowingly used against rats until they are in their third year and have had a considerable amount of experience against rabbits. I say 'knowingly' since rats are sometimes to be found in rabbit burrows. This is just one reason why I will never work any of my ferrets against any animal while the ferrets are wearing muzzles. To do so would be like sending soldiers to fight an enemy armed with blank ammunition. I cannot emphasise too strongly that working ferrets must *never* be muzzled. If you are worried that you may be bitten by your ferrets, then you have not handled them enough and, if you are not handling them regularly, you should not keep them. Well-handled ferrets will not bite, neither will muzzling a ferret help her to do the job better, or even lessen the risk of a lay-up.

During the ferrets' early hunting expeditions, you should be able to form a good idea of their nature and working abilities. It will take a strong, agile, experienced and brave ferret to

Ratting ferrets will find collars a hindrance.

death. Provided that she has been properly handled and taught good manners, this fierceness will not make her any the less manageable or more inclined to bite her handler.

I have found that the best ferrets to use against rats are about thirty centimetres (twelve inches) long (from head to tail), and between two and four years of age. They are never fat, but neither are they skinny, having well proportioned bodies with solid muscle rather than flab. Perhaps surprisingly, they are also usually some of the more placid and easygoing ferrets.

Izzy is just such a ferret. So tame that many people have labelled her as nothing but a 'softy', she often appears to be dozy and lacking any grey matter. However, once she is entered – to either rats or rabbits – her nature changes. It is almost as if a switch has been flicked, letting loose the inner animal, an animal that can move at tremendous speed and with agility. She must have killed hundreds of rats during her career. And now, in the twilight of her life, she can still show the young ferrets a thing or two about hunting rabbits!

Training

Too many books devote huge sections to the subject of training ferrets, whether to work against rabbits or rats. I remember reading one such book many years ago. It contained details of a strict training regime, lasting for many months before the ferret was said to be good enough to tackle rabbits. It would come as no surprise to me if the author had been a Regimental Sergeant Major in an army regiment.

Anyone who has ever had ferrets and tried to work them will tell you that, if the ferret is worthy of the name, she will require no training whatsoever, taking to the job like a duck to water. Wild polecats do not have an instruction manual! If your ferrets have already cut their teeth hunting rabbits, and they possess the necessary maturity and strength, all that is necessary for them to learn how to tackle rats is for you to let them have a go. Do this

tackle rats. Even then, most ferrets only have a rat hunting career of about eighteen months to two years. Once she has received a bad mauling, a ferret will, understandably, be rather reluctant to face rats again. This does not, however, mean that when the ferret is retired from rat duties, she must be made totally redundant; far from it. These ferrets usually make excellent rabbiters and can carry on working for many years.

There is no truth whatsoever in the adage that if you use your ferrets against rats, they will be rendered useless against rabbits. The theory is that your ferrets will become fierce and thus too 'hot' for use against rabbits. Rubbish! All ferrets are 'fierce' when hunting, no matter what the quarry. If she is not, then she will never be any good at working, even against the humble rabbit. In the wild, she would not catch any food, thus starving to

'O.K. Let's get on with the job!'

sensibly, though, by letting them gain rat experience in an area where they are not likely to encounter too many at once. Insurmountable odds are not the way that confidence is built up.

Dogs

Ferreting rats requires the use of at least one, and preferably more, good dogs. Almost without exception, these dogs are terrier types, although not necessarily pedigrees. I have always favoured the Jack Russell, but one of the best ratting dogs that I have seen was a miniature Yorkshire Terrier, complete with pink ribbon on her head! No doubt when she was with her lady owner in the big city she was every bit the toff, but when she was smuggled out of the house to take part in a rat hunt, she became a superb ratter.

This should not, however, come as any great surprise to anyone who knows of the Yorkshire Terrier's past. These little dogs were originally bred to control the rats that were to be found in the Yorkshire coal mines and northern cotton mills. They were also regularly employed by the miners in one of their favourite sports – rat killing contests. These contests involved large numbers of rats being put into a suitable enclosure (very often a deep pit dug in the ground) and dogs being released into the same enclosure. The object of the exercise was to see how many rats a dog could kill in a given amount of time. The Yorkshire Terrier of this era was considerably larger than the ones that we know today. When it was no longer used for sport, in around 1875, it became popular with the upper classes and was deliberately bred smaller so that it could be worn rather like a fashion accessory. The dogs

A rat pit.

were kept up the sleeves of rich ladies of the era and became known as 'sleeve dogs'.

The most important part in the training of any dog is obedience; without it, the dog will never perform as you wish, whether it be a ratting terrier, a gun dog or a guide dog for the blind. Obedience is the corner-stone of all training.

I do not intend to go into the finer points of dog training here; there are plenty of good books on the subject, all readily available (though some better than others). However, it is important to state here that any and every dog that is to be used for ratting must be totally obedient. By that, I mean that the dog will return when called, sit and stay (no matter for how long you wish, nor what temptations are offered up) and be absolutely rock steady with ferrets. This last point should be obvious, but I never fail to marvel at the number of ferreters who feel that they cannot entirely trust their terriers (and other dogs) with their ferrets. If your dogs are not totally steady with the ferrets then, sooner or later, there is going to be big trouble. This could result in either or both sides being injured and, perhaps, your ferrets being killed. You have been warned!

On the first few outings, the dog should be kept under the closest surveillance and corrected immediately if she errs. This does not mean that the dog should be hit or kicked or even chastised in any physical way. I prefer to have my dogs trained so that a good shout, or even just a deep voice, will tell them that I am displeased. If you have a good relationship and rapport with your dog, she will always try to please you, and so will realise that you are not pleased when you shout or speak in a certain manner – it is not what you say, but the way that you say it. Of course, if you have a difficult dog, then this method probably will not work for you but, if the dog is difficult, who is responsible? I am a great believer that there is no such thing as a bad dog, merely bad owners.

By correcting the dog as and when necessary during your hunting excursions, you will train her to do her job well and, within a few months, you should have a dog to be proud of.

Operations

Assuming that you now have your ferrets and your dogs, how do you actually go about hunting rats? As in any hunt, the first thing is to find your quarry. As stated earlier, the brown rat is to be found in many different places, but I would suggest that, to start with at least, you avoid such places as poultry sheds. These places are invariably infested with rats (they live under the floor, coming out to feed on both the chickens and their food) but, until you have gained plenty of experience, these are definitely not the places for you.

My first ratting outing was in a farmer's barn. He was having a clear out of everything in the barn (mainly old, festering bales of hay and straw) and, as he had been having a lot of trouble with rats, had asked a few of his friends to help him and, at the same time, have some excellent sport. There really is no other sport quite so satisfying as rat hunting. I never feel good about killing any of the other quarry that I hunt, in fact, like every true sportsman, I have a high regard for every member of every quarry species.

As the farmer got to the last layer of bales, we (there were about six of us, all with terriers and about a dozen ferrets) released our ferrets down likely holes and put our dogs in good tactical positions, from where they could launch an attack on any rats which escaped the marauding ferrets. Before commencing operations, we had all acquired good, stout sticks (about half a metre (half a yard) long) and taken the precaution of fastening string or elastic bands around our trouser bottoms. This may seem amusing, but rats will run anywhere in order to escape.

Within minutes, the whole place was sheer pandemonium, with ferrets, dogs and rats all chasing each other or seeking places of safety. It was on this day that I discovered that one of the most dangerous things about such ratting operations was not the rats, but the sticks of some of my more excitable colleagues! Some of them swung at rats with gay abandon, while others seemed to become possessed. Rats seem to have that effect on a lot of people.

By the end of that day, we had killed dozens of rats; my ferrets and my terriers had had their first taste of ratting, and we had all had some excellent sport. I was well and truly bitten by the rat hunting bug and, even now, after I have vowed never to risk Weil's Disease again, I still hanker after the excitement that can only be obtained from hunting rats.

11

Ailments

'They do certainly give very strange, and newfangled names to diseases.'

Plato

Ferrets are extremely hardy creatures and, if properly fed and kept in good, clean conditions, they very rarely suffer any malady. Prevention is always better than cure and so you would be well advised to ensure that your ferrets are well looked after on a day-to-day basis. Not only will this mean that the ferrets themselves are happier and healthier, but you will get more out of the ferrets and will not have to keep taking them to the vet.

Some veterinary surgeons now encourage ferret keepers to have their animals inoculated against the more common diseases and some ferreters do this. However, with a few exceptions (such as the vaccination against leptospirosis), I have only once had any of my ferrets treated in this way. This was when I had acquired a young hob that had been bought by a young child at a country fair, from a very unscrupulous vendor. The hob was only about four or five weeks old and should never have been taken away from his mother (twelve weeks is the absolute minimum age at which a ferret kit should be removed from the maternal protector). Further, the child's parents did not want their daughter to have a ferret, although the vendor had managed to persuade the girl (in her parents' absence) that they would not mind.

The parents brought both the weeping child and the young kit to the area where I was giving a display with my own ferrets. They were, quite understandably, very upset and angry at the whole situation that they now found themselves in. At first, they tried to take their frustrations out on me but, when I agreed with them that the sale had been completely reprehensible, they soon calmed down. I do not like taking in too many waifs and strays, and the kit did not look in the best of health but, much against my better judgement, I agreed to take the kit and placed it in the display cage, where it very quickly settled down with my ferrets. Rather pathetically, he tried to suckle from every adult ferret that came his way.

Such episodes can only do harm to the sport in general and are very bad for public relations. Unfortunately, there will always be such unscrupulous people who are willing to try to make a bit of quick cash by selling their animals in such a manner.

Within a few days of returning home, I noticed that the kit was ill. I immediately isolated him and arranged to take him to a vet who I knew had an interest in and knowledge of ferrets. This is an important point, since many vets (too many) unfortunately do not see ferrets often enough to gain any real experience of them. I feel that this is because some people who keep ferrets (I cannot – and will not – refer to them as ferreters, since they do not deserve that title) cannot be bothered to take their sick or injured animals along for treatment. I once spoke to such a person and he told me that he felt that it was a waste of both his time and money to take a ferret to the vet. 'After all,' he said, 'the ferret is only worth a couple of quid, and the vet will charge me more than that just to see it!' Such people are a disgrace to the human race. Perhaps, if the cost of a good working ferret was ever to equal that of a good working terrier, such practices would cease. If that is so, I cannot wait for the day when a ferret will cost £30 or more.

When the vet saw the young hob, he

confirmed my own diagnosis – Distemper. The best thing would be to have the hob put down and a full autopsy performed, in case of other contagious diseases. Meanwhile, I had to protect my other ferrets and so I vaccinated every one of them against Distemper. Luckily, none of the others contracted this disease, and the autopsy confirmed that it was Distemper that had killed the hob, and that there were no other harmful factors present.

This is an all too common happening, where unscrupulous people will sell under age and sickly animals to unsuspecting members of the public. Luckily, such organisations as the National Ferret Welfare Society are now conducting a very effective public relations exercise to educate the public. If you ever see such animals being sold at country fairs or other such occasions, make sure that you tell the event organisers and, if they are there, the local officials of the RSPCA, who will take the appropriate action. Unfortunately, as long as there are people gullible enough to buy animals from these people, they will continue to trade in animal misery.

The foregoing illustrates, I hope, that one can never be too careful about introducing new stock. It is always worth 'quarantining' new animals for a couple of weeks, to ensure that they are not carrying any contagious diseases. Even this, however, is not completely foolproof. If you have obtained your stock from a reputable breeder/keeper, then you need not have too many worries. Always check the conditions that the ferrets are kept in at home and examine them for any signs of illness, such as diarrhoea, discharge from any opening (eyes, anus, etc.), poor coat and

Ferrets kept in good, clean conditions will be less likely to succumb to illness.

lethargy. Avoid such animals at all cost and, after handling them, ensure that you wash your hands well with disinfectant.

As stated earlier, some vets are more *au fait* with ferrets than others. It is always worth making investigations to find the most suitable vet for your animals *before* you require his services. If you experience any trouble obtaining such information, contact the British Small Animal Veterinary Association (*see* Appendix 2), who will do their best to help you. I also recommend that every responsible ferret owner have a copy of *Manual of Exotic Pets* (published by the BSAVA). That the humble ferret appears in a book with such a title indicates that the animal is not considered to be too common in the vet's surgery. As that book lists all of the more specialised treatments and anaesthetics for the vet's benefit, I am not going to waste space here by repeating them. After all, such information is of little use to the lay person, as not only do they not possess the necessary skills and training, but they will also be unable to obtain the relevant drugs. Those who are really interested will, I have no doubt, obtain a copy of the aforementioned book.

First Aid

The most common ferret injuries occur when the animal is being worked. These injuries usually consist of minor cuts and abrasions and, if the ferret is not to suffer any adverse after effects of such injuries, it is advisable that a small first aid kit be taken along on every hunting foray. At the very least, injured ferrets must be given the necessary first aid treatment on their return home.

Contents of Ferret First Aid Kit

Scissors (preferably curved and round ended) To cut off any fur around a wound.
Antiseptic Lotion To cleanse wound and other abrasions.
Antibiotic Powder To apply to wounds after they have been thoroughly cleaned.
Antihistamine For treatment of stings etc.
Tweezers For removal of thorns and other foreign bodies.
Cotton Wool For cleaning wounds etc. and also for stemming the flow of blood.
Bandages A selection of different sized bandages is useful for the treatment of many different types of injury, from wounds to broken limbs.
Surgical Gauze For padding wounds and also stemming the blood flow.
Adhesive Plasters For applying directly to small wounds and also to help keep other dressings and bandages in place.
Cotton Buds For cleaning wounds etc. and for the application of ointments etc.
Table Salt By dissolving two teaspoons of salt in a pint of water, you will obtain a good solution to counter any infection and also wash out any debris from the wound.
Dettox An excellent medium for washing areas around wounds, in order to prevent the influx of more dirt to the wound. It is also good for washing one's own hands after working with any animals.
Alcohol For the removal of ticks etc.
Sodium Bicarbonate Used on a wet compress, this helps to reduce swelling.

Common Injuries and Diseases and their Treatment

Abscesses

Abscesses are simply wounds which have filled with pus. They can be caused by a variety of occurrences, such as bites, cuts or damage to the inside of the mouth, caused by bones in the ferret's diet. In order to prevent wounds developing into abscesses, ensure that the wounds are thoroughly cleaned and disinfected. Once abscesses have developed, they will require lancing and draining, often several times, and it may be necessary for the animal to be given a course of antibiotics. These must be given by a veterinary surgeon.

Alopecia

Hair loss. This is often caused by the feeding of too many raw eggs. This can cause a biotin deficiency which may result in this condition. There are also many other causes of hair loss in ferrets, and it is recommended that any ferrets manifesting such symptoms be given a thorough examination by a qualified vet. (*See also* Mites.)

Bites and Stings

These need to be split into four categories, namely insect, rat, snake and ferret.

Insect Bites (including stings)

Clip a little fur away from the area, so that you can actually see the problem. Then wash with saline solution or Dettox. If there is a sting present, this should be carefully removed with the tweezers and then the area wiped with cotton wool (or a cotton bud) soaked in alcohol, such as surgical spirit. Dry the area and use an antihistamine spray or apply a wet compress; this will reduce the irritation and any swelling.

If the ferret has been bitten or stung in the throat, she should be taken to the vet as soon as possible, as such stings can cause swelling that may block the air ways and thus kill the ferret.

Rat Bites

Rat bites are, potentially, the most dangerous of all bites that a working ferret may suffer. Rats can carry many harmful diseases and it is essential that no risks are taken. Clip away the fur from around the wound, ensuring that the clippings do not become entangled in the wound itself. A vet once suggested using wet scissors as the hairs then stick to the blades rather than falling on to the wound. Clean the area well with a saline solution and then an antiseptic liquid. Apply liberal amounts of antibiotic dusting powder. If the wound is large, or you have good reason to believe that the rat is infected, take the injured ferret to the vet as soon as possible after the injury. I would always recommend this action after any rat bite.

Snake Bites

There is only one venomous snake in Britain (none in Northern Ireland) and that is the adder. Although it is unusual for ferrets or dogs to be bitten by these reptiles, it does sometimes happen. During the spring or early summer, snakes are rather lethargic, especially the gravid (pregnant) females. At such time, they will keep still as long as possible, even when approached. If your ferret or dog does not see the snake and stands on it, the snake will bite. It is most important that you keep the injured animal as calm as possible (you must also remain calm, as your actions will influence the ferret), and seek immediate medical attention.

Adder poison paralyses the victim's system and, if the bite is in the head, neck or chest area, it can prove fatal. A few years ago, while walking with my English Springer Spaniels on a moor in North Wales, Belle, the oldest dog, was bitten on her rear foot when she accidentally stood on a slumbering adder. Within an hour, her foot was bigger than a man's fist. The foot was so swollen, that the vet thought we might have to resort to surgery, as the skin was stretched to its limit and was in danger of splitting. Luckily, this did not happen and, because Belle is such a steady and calm dog, she survived the attack. As an illustration of the paralysing effects of the adder's venom, when Belle vomited about forty-eight hours after the bite, she brought back the food (completely undigested) that she had eaten about an hour before the attack.

Ferret Bites

Although it may not at first seem so obvious, ferrets are more likely to suffer from bites from other ferrets than from any other animal. This is especially so during the breeding season, when the hob takes hold of the jill by the scruff, hanging on tightly and, very often, breaking her skin with his teeth. These types of injuries are not usually serious, providing that they are given first aid treatment.

The area must be clipped of fur and then the wound thoroughly washed with a saline solution and then with an antiseptic liquid. A good dusting with an antibiotic wound powder will finish the job. If this action is not taken, the wound may fester and result in an abscess.

Breathing Problems

Ferrets gasping for breath are obviously showing symptoms of some form of breathing difficulty. This may be heatstroke, fluid on the lungs or an obstruction of some kind. Many obstructions can be removed from a ferret's mouth with a cotton bud or even a finger. Artificial respiration, though difficult, is possible with ferrets. Do not blow too hard, as you may cause irreparable damage to the animal's lungs. If the symptoms persist, or you cannot find the cause, seek medical advice.

Botulism

Botulism is probably the biggest killer of ferrets today. The disease is caused by one of the most common bacterium known to science, *Clostridium botulinum* (usually 'Type C'). When this bacterium comes into contact with any decaying flesh (i.e. meat), a deadly toxin is formed. If this flesh is then eaten by an animal (in our case a ferret), this toxin affects its victim by attacking the animal's nervous system, causing paralysis, usually in the hind legs at first. Eventually, this paralysis will affect the body's vital organs, causing death. There is no cure for this disease.

In order to try to prevent this deadly disease, pay particular attention to the meat that you feed; defrost frozen meat and feed immediately. If there is any doubt whatsoever about the meat, boil it for at least fifteen minutes before feeding. Botulism is not contagious and sometimes only one animal of a group may succumb to the illness.

Convulsions

Convulsions are often an indication that the ferret has an infection of some kind or has been poisoned; they are not, in themselves, a disease. One of the most common causes in captive ferrets is heatstroke, or the 'sweats'.

Dental Problems

Ferrets occasionally damage their teeth, either while working or even in their cage when chewing the wire mesh or, perhaps, the food dish. Gingivitis, a gum disorder, is also quite common. Both conditions must be treated by a properly qualified vet. Some vets are reluctant to work inside a ferret's mouth without first putting the animal under an anaesthetic, no matter how tame the owner may say the animal is.

Diarrhoea

Diarrhoea in ferrets (often referred to as the 'scours') is very often merely a sign that the animal has been fed on a poor diet. Feeding milk sops and/or eggs, too much fat, a sudden and abrupt change of diet and food which has gone off all have this effect. Diarrhoea can also be indicative of some other, more serious affliction, such as poisoning, internal parasites or even stress.

If you are feeding your ferrets as I have suggested, they should not suffer from loose motions as a matter of course (which they almost certainly would if they were fed on a bread and milk diet), and so you should take note of anything that you have fed them, or that has happened, that is out of the ordinary.

In order to arrest diarrhoea (which, if not treated can cause the animal to dehydrate and, perhaps, die), you should isolate the affected ferret or ferrets and keep them on a water only regime for twenty-four hours, dosing with kaolin solution at regular intervals (about every couple of hours). After the fast, food intake should be gradually built up again, otherwise the whole problem may recur. If the diarrhoea persists, or if there is blood in the motions, the vet must be consulted.

Distemper

Canine distemper, to give it its full name, is a virus and is one of the most common fatal diseases in ferrets. Many owners now have their animals vaccinated against this disease, as a matter of course. If you are considering this, you should consult with your own vet, who will advise you accordingly.

Symptoms of the disease are swollen feet (ultimately leading to Hard Pad, the thickening of the soles of the feet and a classical sign of Distemper infection), runny eyes and nose, diarrhoea, lack of appetite, a larger than average thirst and a rash, usually under the chin. In its latter stages, the infected animal will vomit, have convulsions and, shortly before dying, will pass into a coma.

At the first signs of Distemper, any infected ferrets must be isolated, as the disease is highly contagious. Ensure that your hands are thoroughly disinfected after handling any sick animal (dogs can also contract this disease, as the name suggests). Seek immediate veterinary advice, but it is worth noting that only very mild cases can be treated. It is often kinder, both to the infected ferrets and the others in your care, if the infected ferret is put down once the diagnosis is confirmed.

Enteritis

If your ferrets show signs of blood in their diarrhoea, this probably indicates a form of enteritis. This can be caused by several different things but, usually, it is the bacterium *Escherichia coli* (often referred to as *E. coli* and formerly known to science as *Bacillus coli*). The immediate treatment with a broad spectrum antibiotic, supplemented with regular doses of kaolin, may cure this condition. If left untreated, the affected animal will die.

Ferrets can also be affected by Feline Enteritis Virus (Panleukopenia). This causes an acute haemorrhagic enteritis, usually fatal.

It may be possible to vaccinate ferrets against this virus (using cat vaccine), but this would need confirmation from the manufacturers of the vaccine; your vet will advise you.

Foot Rot

Not so many years ago, this affliction was quite prevalent and thought to be caused solely by the ferrets being kept in dirty, wet conditions. While these types of conditions will do nothing to help the ferrets' health, they are not in themselves solely responsible for foot rot. The culprit is a mite, *Sarcoptes scabiei*.

The symptoms of foot rot are swollen, scabby feet. If left untreated, the claws will eventually drop off. Affected animals must be isolated at once and all other ferrets examined closely. All bedding and wood shavings must be removed from the cage and burned. The cage itself must be thoroughly cleaned out with a strong solution of bleach (this must be completely rinsed off before any ferrets are returned to the cage). All infected ferrets must be taken to a vet at once. Home treatment is very rarely effective, and time waited is time wasted.

Heatstroke (the 'sweats')

Ferrets react very badly to too much heat and this must always be borne in mind. The siting of the cage (as discussed in an earlier chapter) is very important, but so too is the position that they are left in while out working. In the confines of a carrying box, the temperature can soon rise, even in the cooler sunshine of autumn and spring. This is even more dangerous if the ferrets are left in a car for any length of time. Remember that the sun does not stay in the same position throughout the day, and that, even if the box or car is in the shadows when you leave it, it may not stay that way for long.

In extreme summer temperatures, when it is not possible to keep the ferret's cub or court as cool as one would like, wet cloths may be hung over the cage to keep the temperature down.

Do remember that they will soon dry out, and so will require constant attention throughout the day.

The first signs of the sweats (a rather misleading term, since ferrets cannot sweat) is an agitated ferret in obvious distress. They usually stretch out in their cages and will pant heavily, although this panting has very little cooling effect. If left untreated, they will eventually collapse, pass into a coma and, ultimately, die.

You must act immediately that one of your ferrets shows these symptoms. Delay can be fatal. The ferret's body is overheating, and so your first task must be to lower her body temperature. I find that the best method is to literally dunk the animal into a bucket of cold water. Do not totally immerse for more than a few seconds. Repeat this procedure regularly for the next few minutes, by which time (hopefully) the ferret will be showing signs of recovery.

At this stage, place the ferret in a cage that is in a cool position and, for about the next hour (or until the ferret appears to be fully re-covered), keep sprinkling cold water on the animal's head and back. It is most important to keep the head cool, since brain death can occur, as the brain is quite literally 'pickled'. Veterinary advice should be sought at the earliest opportunity.

Influenza

Ferrets cannot catch the flu from their owners, or vice versa. 'Flu viruses are usually species specific. Symptoms in humans and ferrets are about the same – fever, sneezing and lack of appetite. Keep infected ferrets isolated and generally nurse the patient who, almost in-variably, will recover.

Leukaemia

This disease very occasionally appears in ferrets but, in most cases, is almost completely undetectable until the ferrret is almost at death's door. The presence of any lumps in the animal's groin or abdomen, or under the jaw may indicate this disease. Medical advice should be sought immediately.

Mastitis

This is the inflammation of the jill's mammary glands. Obviously, this can only occur when the jill is feeding young but it is a very painful condition that requires immediate medical attention. The glands become very swollen and hard and the kits obtain very little – if any – milk. Unless it is cleared up quickly, the kits will probably die and the jill will, at best, be very ill. The disease is caused by bacterial infection and treatment usually consists of antibiotics.

Mites

Mites come in many different breeds and sizes; all of them have unpleasant effects on the ferret. The commonest problem caused by mites is mange. Ferrets can become infected by coming into direct contact with other infected animals (alive or dead, e.g. rodents that are fed to the ferrets) or simply by being on infected ground. The first sign is persistent scratching, even though there is no obvious cause such as fleas. Eventually, the skin will become very red and sore, a symptom that is readily noticed in albino ferrets. As the disease progresses, these sores cause baldness and the sores become even worse.

Benzyl Benzoate, a cream available from your local vet or even from the chemist, should be applied to the affected areas but not all areas at once, as the cream will block the skin's pores. Leave the cream on each affected area for about twenty-four hours and then wash off, repeating after forty-eight hours. Re-member to treat the cage thoroughly too, soaking it in a strong solution of disinfectant or bleach, which must be washed off before any ferret is returned to the cage. If the symptoms persist, seek veterinary advice. Be warned! Mange can be contracted by humans.

Ear mites are quite common in ferrets and, if

your ferrets seem to spend a lot of time scratching their ears, an investigation is called for. A build up of wax in the ears, dotted with black specks, is a sure indication that ferrets have ear mites (these black specks are probably spots of dried blood; ear mites are usually white or colourless and are not visible to the naked eye – a magnifying lens or otoscope is required). If left untreated the mites will cause the ferret to scratch, sometimes until her ears actually bleed. The mites may also move down the aural canal and infect the middle ear. Such an infection will cause the afflicted animal to lose her sense of balance. This may be indicated either by the ferret being unable to hold her head straight or, in more serious cases, by constantly falling over.

Veterinary advice must be sought at once. Your vet will probably prescribe ear drops, to be administered on a regular basis over the next few weeks. It is important that all ferrets that have been in contact with the infected ferret are also treated, as ear mites can infect other animals who may not show any symptoms for some time.

Paralysis

Often caused by injury, paralysis can also be inherited. If the latter is the case, the disorder will show itself in young litters. There is usually no cure for this and it is, therefore, best to have the animals destroyed. The parents of such litters should not be used for breeding again, as it is obvious that at least one (and probably both) is carrying the genetic defect responsible for this complaint.

If an adult ferret develops any paralysis, this is usually an indication of injury (especially if the animal has been working recently, or climbing) or the later signs of tuberculosis or even a stroke. Veterinary attention and advice must be sought immediately.

Parasites

Even the most pampered ferrets can suffer from the unwanted attentions of parasites, either internal or external. Ferrets occasionally suffer from worms, passed on from their food source (rabbits are often infected with tapeworms).

The first signs of a worm infection in your ferrets is an insatiable appetite coupled with a loss of weight. Often, segments of the worms will be found in the ferret's faeces before other symptoms indicate a problem. All worm infestations can be treated with modern medicines but, as the ferret is much smaller than a dog, do not try to treat the animal with powders in doses that your local pet shop may recommend for a dog. Seek expert medical advice.

Fleas, ticks and sometimes (though rarely) lice, are external parasites that most working ferrets will catch at some stage of their career. Fleas and lice can be easily dealt with by using a good quality powder or spray designed for the job. Remember to remove all of the bedding and wood shavings from the ferret's cage and then treat the cage itself with the powder, otherwise the problem will keep recurring. These powders and sprays must not, however, be used where a jill is still feeding her kits, as there is a danger of poisoning the litter.

Ticks are rather more difficult to deal with, but they do respond to some sprays and powders (only available from veterinary surgeons). Never pull ticks out, as their mouthparts will remain in the ferret's flesh,

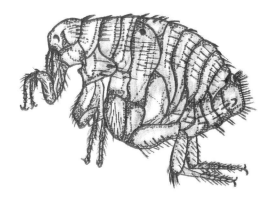

The flea.

The louse.

The tick.

probably eventually causing an abscess. Paint alcohol, such as surgical spirit, on the tick using a fine paint brush. Within twenty-four hours, the tick should have died and dropped off. If it has not, simply repeat the process.

Although some old hands (and even some books) suggest that ticks be burned off with a lighted cigarette, this should never be attempted. It is all too easy to burn the ferret with the cigarette and the alcohol method is much more effective, with none of the dangers.

Ringworm

Occasionally evident in ferrets, this disease is probably transmitted by infected cats. The condition manifests itself with hair loss and bald, scaly patches of skin. The disease, despite its name, is not caused by worms – it is a fungal infection. Home treatment is sometimes successful, but it is strongly recommended that veterinary advice is sought. It must be treated immediately, as the condition is transmissible to man.

Sarcoptic Mange

A disease caused by the mite *Sarcoptes scabei*. In man, the condition is known as scabies. (*See also* Mites.)

Shock

Shock, which is an acute fall in blood pressure, is often evident after the ferret has been involved in an accident or has been injured or, in fact, almost any severe trauma. It manifests itself by all or some of the following symptoms: cool skin and pale lips and gums (lack of circulation), faint, rapid pulse, and staring eyes.

The victim must be kept warm and her blood circulation returned to normal as soon as possible. This is best done by gently massaging the ferret (to help circulation) and wrapping her in a towel or blanket, to keep her warm. Keep the animal quiet and warm and contact your vet.

Tuberculosis

Ferrets are susceptible to several kinds of tuberculosis – avian, bovine and human. Symptoms include paralysis of the limbs, diarrhoea and wasting of the body. Almost always fatal, the disease is highly contagious and, if you suspect your stock might be infected, contact your vet at once.

Without a shadow of a doubt, the best way to ensure healthy ferrets is to indulge in good husbandry. Ferrets have the disturbing habit of often not showing any symptoms until they are almost dead. If you suspect any of your stock of sickening, contact your veterinary surgeon without delay.

12

On the Fringe

'If a ferret bites you, it is nearly always your own fault.'
Phil Drabble

It is well known that ferrets are used for hunting rabbits, rats and some other animals. It is also now quite widely accepted that ferrets make excellent pets. This is especially true in the United States of America, where it is illegal in most States to use the ferret for any type of hunting. There are, however, various other uses to which ferrets have been put quite successfully.

Pets

To the uninitiated, ferrets would seem to be one of the most unlikely pets. According to their critics, ferrets smell, are completely untameable and cannot be trusted. If you have read the contents of this book, I am sure that you will now know that I do not hold these beliefs. Neither, it would seem, do many other pet keepers who have discovered the charms of *Mustella putorius furo*. It is a fact that ferrets are fast becoming one of the more popular of the unusual pets that today's society seems to crave.

It is not the intention of this chapter, or even of this book, to persuade people to keep ferrets. Like all animals, ferrets require a lot of looking after, which requires time, effort and money (for food and housing, not to mention vets' bills). No animal should ever be bought on a whim, and certainly not a ferret.

Too many people breed surplus stock every year, which they then palm off to unsuspecting members of the public, often young children. Once the full implication of keeping ferrets has sunk in, I am sure that many of these ferrets are dumped – a reprehensible action, but not one

that is confined merely to ferrets. Witness the number of cats and dogs that are abandoned each year and end up in the hands of the RSPCA, many to be destroyed because of lack of space. It is to be hoped that potential ferret keepers will read this and other books, from cover to cover, in order to see just what they are letting themselves in for, *before* they acquire their ferrets. In this way they will see just what pleasures, hard work and expense they are likely to let themselves in for. After that, the decision can be made as to whether or not to purchase any ferrets. All such decisions should always be made only after one has all of the facts.

Ferrets have a lot to offer as pets; their size is such that they can be easily handled, even by quite young children, and yet they do not require huge living areas. They can be given the run of the house, providing that the human occupants are careful where they put their feet. Ferrets have extremely clean habits, and it is relatively easy to train them to use a litter tray, in much the same way as a family cat. It is said that a home with a ferret or two in it, is less likely to be subjected to an invasion of mice and/or rats, and it is certainly true that members of the *Mustelidae* are kept as household pets for just that purpose in many parts of the world.

Ferrets can also be taken for walks! This can either be on the end of a collar and lead or even in one's pocket. Izzy loves nothing more than curling up in the pocket of my jacket. At country shows where we give displays, she is constantly climbing into the pockets of perfect strangers when I put her on the table top for the crowds to see and touch. She does not seem to mind whose pocket it is, she just loves pockets in general!

Those keepers who put their ferrets on a lead will use either a collar or a harness. These are made from soft leather and available from country sports shops and even from many pet shops – another sign that the ferret's popularity as a pet is on the increase. Just like a dog or cat, ferrets need to become accustomed to the collar and then the lead. It is advisable to put the collar on so that it is just too tight to be pulled over the ferret's head, but not too tight to cause it any discomfort. Once the collar is fitted, the ferret should be distracted – by either food or play – and then it will accept the collar quite easily. Collars should never be left on when the ferret is given exercise off the lead, as the animal may well end up hanging herself.

Once the ferret has become used to the collar and fully accepts it, attach the lead and leave it trailing while you, once again, distract the ferret's attention from the encumbrance. Within a very short time, your ferret will not bother about the collar and lead, and then you can start to take her for walks. Always remember that not everyone will share your enthusiasm for ferrets. Bear in mind, too, that the ferret is quite small and human feet have a habit of being big and clumsy. In a human foot versus ferret combat, the ferret will always come out worse.

For normal transport, a cat carying box or one of the many ferret carrying boxes, sold by country sports shops, is recommended. This will ensure that your ferret always has a safe, warm means of transport – important if your pet should ever take ill or is injured. Again, it is important that all of your ferrets become used to being transported in this way, and so the animals must be completely accustomed to the box before it is ever needed. The best way to do this is to allow the ferrets to play in and around the box, perhaps putting small edible

A pet ferret fitted with a harness will enjoy being taken for a walk.

titbits inside the box, in order to persuade them that there is nothing to fear.

The housing of pet ferrets differs tremendously from one keeper to the other. I believe that ferrets should be kept outside, preferably in a court, with plenty of fresh air and room to exercise. Some pet keepers, however, allow their ferrets to live in the home, wherever the ferret desires. This practice has many inherent dangers. Ferrets can get into all kinds of places, including cupboards housing electric meters or into refrigerators containing milk, eggs and meat! After having seen the chaos left behind by a fridge-raiding ferret, I can tell you that the cleaning up (and replacement of food) was not completed in five minutes!

Pet ferrets have also found their way into washing machines, linen baskets and wardrobes. I have heard reports that some ferrets manage to injure themselves (often fatally) during their jaunts around the home. Be warned! I strongly suggest that all ferrets, when not under the direct supervision and watchful eyes of their owners, are kept confined to their quarters. They can certainly be given the run of the human home when there is someone around to watch them, but not at other times.

The housing of pet ferrets can be identical to that used for working ferrets (*see* Chapter 3). However, many owners of pet ferrets like to have their charges living in a cage in the home. In this case, one of the many hutches sold for rabbits and guinea pigs would be suitable. Most of these cages are of a rather flimsy construction and hardly ever painted. This is a job that should be done before the ferret is housed in the hutch, as it will prevent

Even pet ferrets can live out of doors.

urine and other fluids from soaking into the wood. Plastic is now also commonly used for cage construction and, as long as the hutch is kept indoors and away from the elements, this is also satisfactory. Plastic and fibreglass hutches must never be used out of doors, as they offer very little protection against the elements and hardly any insulation against extremes of temperature.

Born escapologists, ferrets will make their escape through the most unlikely – and seemingly impossible – opening. Gaps in the skirting board or floorboards have a magnetic attraction for ferrets. Even Houdini would have had a deep respect for the ferret's ability to find an escape route from almost any room or building. If you do lose a ferret, employ the services of several live-catch traps (such as those marketed for mink), baited with a little of the ferret's favourite food. These should be placed all around the room or building from which the escape was made, especially in the area in which it is suspected that the ferret found her escape route.

Ferrets are hoarders. They will hoard almost anything that they can carry to a suitable hiding place – shiny buttons, coins, cutlery, items of clothing (socks are a particular favourite) and countless other household items.

Whether kept as workers or as pets, ferrets should never be sentenced to solitary confinement. They like the company of their own species, even though the wild polecat does lead a rather solitary existence. Many pet keepers seem to prefer hobs to jills and, if this is the case and breeding is not on the agenda, then a couple of hobbles (vasectomised hobs) will make excellent pets. These animals will also be much in demand to service the jills of other keepers, who do not wish their animals to have litters, but do not want to risk the possible medical problems of their jills remaining in season for several months.

Pet owners, irrespective of the species that they own, always seem to want to give their pets some toys to play with. With ferrets, these toys can range from ones specifically manu-

factured for such animals as cats (e.g. 'kelly' toys or imitation mice, sometimes on wheels) to such everyday household items as paper bags and cardboard boxes. Table tennis balls are a particular favourite. Tubes, either cardboard or plastic, are another source of amusement and objects hanging on the end of a piece of string will have exactly the same effect on a pet ferret as they would on a cat.

Ferrets in Industry

Ferrets have been put to many uses in industry, most utilising their ability (and willingness) to pass through long, narrow piping and into confined places. One ferret was used to carry a line through tunnels in the Palace of Westminster, in order that cables could be hauled through those tunnels. The cables were for television cameras filming the wedding of H.R.H. the Prince of Wales and Lady Diana Spencer.

Ferrets have been used for this type of work for many years, particularly in the United States of America. They have been used for carrying lines through oil pipes and this eventually led to their use in racing.

Ferret Racing

As previously stated, American oil men used ferrets for hauling lines through pipes and, in order to relieve the tedium of their jobs and the long days and nights that they spent away from home, they looked to the ferret to supply them with some amusement. Taking the ferret's job just one step further, the oil men set up lengths of piping and held races for the ferrets. Within a few years, this sport had spread over the US, and it was only a short time before it crossed the Atlantic to Britain.

Here it was quickly realised that not only was this a very enjoyable sport for the onlookers, it was good fun for the ferrets, too. The spectator potential was realised, and it was not long before ferret racing was a

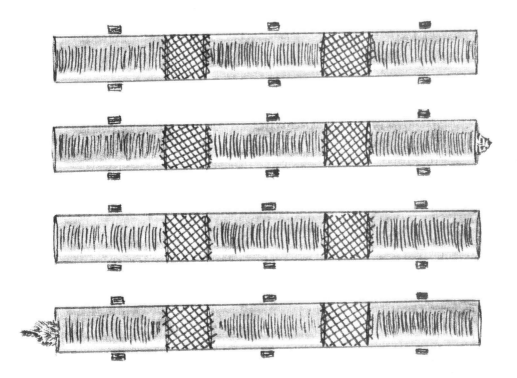

Plan of a ferret race, showing the layout of pipes.

popular event staged at almost every country fair, a phenomenon that owes much to the efforts of the National Ferret Welfare Society (NFWS).

Today, the NFWS and its affiliated clubs not only organise such events, but also lay down guidelines – they do not like to think of them as rules – for the races themselves. Although not all ferret races are identical, they all follow these guidelines and so the following is offered as a rough guide to how such an event is organised.

The course itself consists of several (usually three or more) lengths of pipe, tubing, conduit or some similar material. The shape and diameter of this pipe is immaterial, being quite large bore and square in shape, to narrow and circular. The total length of this piping is not stipulated, but is usually between four and six metres (four and six yards) in total length. Between each piece of pipe is an area of approximately twenty centimetres (eight

Ferret racing is good fun – for humans and ferrets!

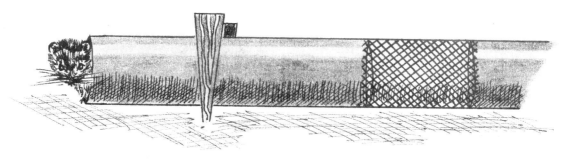

A ferret emerging from a pipe during a race.

inches) covered with chicken mesh or other such material.

There are usually between four and six separate tunnels like this. The object is to introduce a ferret into one end of the tunnel and, when the tip of her tail has left the other end, the owner has to run there and turn his ferret around for the return journey. At one time, the owner was allowed to run to the far end of the tunnel immediately that he had entered his ferret. Here, he would encourage the ferret by whatever means at his disposal, apart from physically touching the ferret. This is no longer allowed, and the ferret must run the course of her own volition.

The first ferret to completely emerge from the end of the tunnel after the second leg, is the winner of that heat but, as the race is against the clock, with the four fastest ferrets competing against each other in the finals, this does not necessarily mean that the winner of a heat will have the opportunity to race again.

So popular did this sport become that it was thought that breeders would begin to produce ferrets specifically designed to compete. This, fortunately, has not proved to be the case, and the main reason that ferrets are kept and bred is for hunting the rabbit. Ferret racing is fun, and should never be seen as anything else.

Fur Farming

Ferrets, along with other members of their tribe, such as mink, have been farmed for their fur (known as 'fitch'), a practice that still exists in some countries, notably New Zealand. It is not the intention of this book to advocate the keeping of ferrets for this purpose.

Laboratories

Laboratories in Britain and other countries have used the ferret in experiments, most notably in the quest for a cure for the common cold and influenza. Some people will breed their ferrets to supply the demand for these institutes, but I cannot encourage this, important as the research may be.

Ferret Legging

This is a sport indulged in by some ferret keepers, notably in the north of England, especially around Barnsley, in South Yorkshire. The sport probably originated from the habit of poachers who had to keep their ferrets out of sight of curious policemen, during any nefarious excursions. To do this, the poachers would hide the ferrets in their clothing, often down their trouser legs, which were always worn either tucked into their boots or, as most of them rode bicycles, with bicycle clips.

Today, the sport is usually held at charity events, to raise money for some good cause – which is the only good thing that can be said for it. The man (and it is usually only men who participate in such competitions) is expected to put a ferret (undrugged, not wearing a muzzle and with all of her teeth intact) down his trousers from the top. His trouser bottoms are tied and he is not allowed to wear any underclothes! The winner is the man who can endure this for the longest length of time.

Bites to the humans are common, and I feel sure that this is because of the stress and fear to which the ferret participants are subjected. The sport is not to be recommended!

Shows

Like many small animals, ferrets are often exhibited and compared against each other on the show bench. These ferret shows, mainly organised by the National Ferret Welfare Society and its affiliated clubs, take place throughout the summer months at venues (usually country shows) all around Britain.

There are no real rules for the judging of ferrets, but I tend to use the same principles employed when judging other livestock. The criteria are good condition, ease of handling, quality of fur and cleanliness. I score each of these categories from a maximum of ten points. If, at the end of the show, I have a tie for first place, I simply choose the ferret that I would most like to take home (not that I ever get the opportunity!) Most judges follow a similar procedure.

13

The Law

'Where law ends, tyranny begins.'
William Pitt

The law in general is very complex and constantly changing; this statement also applies to the laws relating to country sports and the keeping of animals. Ignorance of the law, as everyone knows, is no excuse for not abiding by it. It behoves everyone who keeps, breeds, sells or works ferrets to ensure that all of their actions are legal.

Ferret keepers may well find problems with local bylaws as well. Some Acts give specific powers to councils (both local and county) to create bylaws to cover the public's rights of access, as well as the activities that may be carried out on particular pieces of land. Just to add to all of the confusion, the laws in Scotland are very often different to those in England and Wales.

It is not my intention to try to give the authoritative guide to the law as it pertains to ferreters; others have already attempted this, in particular Charlie Parkes and John Thornley, in their book *Fair Game*. A copy of this book belongs on the bookshelves of every person who ever indulges in country sports. Another book worth reading, if not actually buying, is *An Introduction to Animal Law* by Margaret E. Cooper LL B. It should, however, be borne in mind that many such books are out of date before they are published, such is the way with the law. In the following pages, I have attempted to give a broad outline of some of the legal requirements and considerations that ferret owners need to be aware of. Of necessity, much of it is simplified, and the reader is advised to check on the full legal interpretation of any part of the law which he feels might affect him.

Perhaps it would be as well to look at the laws relating to the keeping of ferrets. At the moment, ferrets are not covered by the Dangerous Wild Animals Act, 1976, but more and more species are being added to the list of animals covered by this Act, and it may not be too long before ferrets appear. The Act was originally intended to control and limit the possession of such animals as lions, tigers and venomous snakes by the general public. It came at a time when it was cheaper, and often easier, to buy a lion cub than it was to buy a pedigree dog. Such animals were kept in totally unsuitable accommodation and, in many cases, posed a serious threat to the safety of the general public.

If the ferret ever was included, this would mean licensing by the Local Authority, who would have to be satisfied that you were a suitable person to possess your animal, you had suitable accommodation and that your keeping them would not cause a public nuisance.

The owner of an animal has certain legal obligations, such as limiting the damage or nuisance (noise, smell, etc.) that they cause. In the eyes of the Law, the owner is not necessarily the person who has ownership in its accepted sense. The person who borrows, or even looks after, a ferret may be classed as the owner and he then becomes liable for complying with the statutory requirements governing the keeping and use of the ferret.

As the ferret is classed as a 'domestic animal', it can be owned by a person in exactly the same way that a car or other inanimate object can. Wild animals, such as rabbits, on the other hand, belong to no one, because, under statute law (Theft Act, 1968), they are not classed as property. This does not, however, mean that anyone can take these animals – because of this peculiar situation poaching becomes an offence. It is defined in *Stone's Justices' Manual* as 'the offence committed by a person who pursues, kills or takes certain game birds and animals on land where he has no right'. These 'certain gamebirds and animals' were defined by the Poaching Prevention Act, 1862. The list includes the rabbit, the only game species that concerns the ferreter.

Thus, the rabbit is classed as game or, to be more precise, 'ground game'. Yet under the Pests Act, 1954, it is also classed as vermin. The occupier of any land is specifically obliged to control rabbits under this Act, or, at the very least, to prevent them from causing damage. Any occupier who fails to fulfill these obligations may be prosecuted or be obliged to pay the bill for someone else to do the work.

Previous to the Ground Game Act, 1880, tenants of land were not allowed to kill ground game, including rabbits. As rabbits caused a great deal of damage to their crops, the farmers were not too pleased. This Act gave the tenant the right to control all ground game on his property. Even if another person also has the specific right to take ground game (e.g. the owner or the person who owns the sporting rights), the occupier still has the right himself. This is known as a concurrent right and the tenant is, in these circumstances, restricted in the manner in which he may take ground game, i.e. only the occupier and one other person may use firearms (including shotguns) against ground game. This is a point worth considering if you are thinking of shooting rabbits over ferrets and asking a few friends along to help.

Although most ferreters may not realise it, there is a close season for rabbits, but only those on moorland and otherwise unenclosed land. On such land, it is an offence (under the Ground Game Act, 1880, as amended by the Ground Game (Amended) Act, 1906) to take or kill ground game between 1 April and 31 August. It is also an offence to use firearms

Rabbits are classed as 'ground game'.

(including shotguns) to kill or injure ground game between 1 September and 10 December. (This latter prohibition can be waived, if all concerned parties agree.)

It should be obvious by now, that it is extremely easy for a ferreter to fall foul of the law, in his ignorance and without any malice. However, as stated earlier, ignorance is no excuse. Some people, nevertheless, set out to deliberately flout the law. One of the main reasons for this is frustration. Many people buy ferrets, believing that they will easily obtain the necessary permission from some farmer who is desperate to rid himself of a rabbit problem. Some people even think that the farmer will be willing to pay for the service. How wrong can you be. It is a fact of life that there are not enough opportunities around for every interested party to be able to indulge in the sport of ferreting rabbits (which is one reason why so many turn their attentions to ratting).

After many months of fruitless searching, the would-be ferreter becomes more and more frustrated with the situation and, when he sees an area where there is obviously a profusion of rabbits, he decides to risk all and indulges in that age-old pastime of poaching. Anyone who does so is breaking the law, for poaching is just a legal term for a different kind of theft. Such people will, quite rightly, receive their just desserts when (and it is 'when', and not 'if') they are apprehended.

Even so-called common land is usually owned by someone. (It is still poaching to take 'game' on the roadside or verge.) While it is not an offence (yet!) to go 'equipped for poaching', once you are on the land and have set your nets and/or entered a ferret, you are committing an offence, if you do not have the specific permission of the relevant person.

Obtaining Permission to Ferret

How does one obtain permission to ferret, and from whom? To answer the last part of the question first, the only person who can give permission for the pursuit of ground game on his land, is the occupier or owner of that land. In some cases, this permission is given to another person in the shooting (or sporting) rights, and that person may give, or sell, permission to a third party providing that this is allowed in the original agreement from the owner or occupier.

It is always worthwhile obtaining any such permission in writing, and always ensuring that you take along this important piece of evidence on every hunting foray on that land. Without it, you may well find yourself accompanying a police officer to the station, where you will then have to wait until the police are satisfied that you really do have permission – not too serious, but annoying and a waste of good ferreting time.

Obtaining permission to ferret is often gained more by good luck than anything else. I have always found that the best way is to do a favour for a farmer, or even one of his friends or relatives. Then, when the farmer is asking how he can ever repay you, tell him not to worry, and then casually mention the fact that you have seen rabbits on his property and you would even be willing to clear them with your ferrets. This ploy has worked for me on several occasions, although on others I have had to put a lot more effort into the negotiations.

Many farmers, while willing to allow you to use ferrets will not allow the use of guns of any kind. I often feel that, if I was a landowner, I would be very reluctant to allow anyone to walk across my land with a potentially lethal weapon, or at least not until I knew that I could trust them completely.

One way in which I know several acquaintances have obtained ferreting rights (and, in some cases, shooting rights) is by joining the Young Farmer's Club. There are usually local clubs in most areas and, if you are prepared to play your part in the activities of the club, you may be offered the opportunity to participate in some sport. Do not demand sporting rights from members on your first attendance. Take your time; let the members get to know you, and then, casually, drop the matter of ferrets

He has permission to ferret. Do you?

and rabbit hunting into a relevant conversation.

I have often found that, once permission is granted in one area, providing that you do a good job and act sensibly at all times, other avenues quickly open up to you. At one time, I had enough ferreting to fully occupy me for seven days per week, around the year. Even if I could have afforded the time, I doubt that I could have stood the pace!

Once you have obtained permission, do not act outside of the agreement. For instance, many ferreters invite their friends along on ferreting expeditions. Always remember that the farmer has only given permission to you to ferret on his land. While he may not object to you occasionally taking along one friend, he will not be too happy to see a regular attendance by yourself and six or seven friends.

There are other reasons for not inviting friends along on ferreting trips, one of them being poaching. I know of several ferreters who have invited along other kindred spirits to help with their rabbit clearing duties. Some of these have had no problems but one or two found that their 'friend' had been visiting the area on their own, and clearing out all of the rabbits. Nothing is more liable to break up old friendships. Ferreting rights are sacrosanct!

The Wildlife and Countryside Act, 1981

This Act, along with the Wildlife and Countryside (Amendment) Act, 1985, is one of the most important parts of the law relating to British wildlife. There are several specific parts of this Act which will concern the ferreter.

The first point worth considering is Section 14(1) of the Act which states that it is an offence to allow any animal 'which is not ordinarily a resident in Great Britain' to escape. Some authorities are of the opinion that the domesticated ferret (as opposed to the polecat) would qualify as such a creature. I cannot find any reports of such a prosecution taking place, but would recommend that ferrets never be allowed to escape into the wild at any time.

Care must be taken too, to ensure that no badgers are disturbed during ferreting. Although experienced ferreters will be able to identify and differentiate rabbit holes from badger holes (entrances to badger setts are far larger than those to rabbit burrows; the latter

will also have evidence of rabbit faeces in the immediate vicinity), some newcomers may not. This is no excuse for entering any animal to a badger sett. Such action rightly carries heavy (perhaps not heavy enough) penalties. If there is any doubt in your mind as to the species inhabiting a hole, do not enter any animal until you have checked with the landowner and received positive proof that you are unlikely to encounter badgers. Following an amendment to the Badgers Act, 1973, a person found digging at a badger sett would have to prove to the satisfaction of the Court, that they were not digging for a badger. Thus, the onus of proof lies with the defence, rather than the prosecution. Badger digging is a filthy act that needs stamping out. I would not like to see any thug carrying out this obscene act and using ferreting as an excuse.

Providing that you have the appropriate authority, you do not need a Game Licence to take rabbits with ferrets.

Licences

A Game Licence is not required to take rabbits by the use of ferrets, providing that you have authority to be on the land for that purpose.

Guns

The law relating to the use of rifles, shotguns and air rifles is extremely complex and, at the time of writing (May 1988), the law is about to be changed. It is such a complicated area that even many police officers do not fully under-stand the law relating to firearms. Consequently, I do not intend to cover this aspect in too much detail. Specific questions should be directed to the Firearms Department at the British Association for Shooting and Conservation (BASC, formerly known as WAGBI), whose address can be found at the end of this book.

Trespass (being on another person's land without permission or good reason) is not a criminal offence, merely a civil one. Trespass with a gun (armed trespass) is. A person so doing could well find himself under arrest.

14

Lapin Gastronomie

'That all softening, over powering knell,
The tocsin of the soul – the dinner bell.'
Lord Byron

The end product of ferreting (at least ferreting for rabbits) should be food for you and your family. Rabbit meat, although not as popular today as it was in the pre-myxomatosis days, is very tasty and can be cooked in a variety of ways. However, after the rabbits are caught and before they can be eaten, they must be prepared for the pot.

Gutting a Rabbit

Immediately on death, or as soon after as is feasible, the rabbits must have their bladders emptied of urine. This task, known as 'peeing', or as 'thumbing' (because of the action of the thumbs), is a simple operation where the rabbit is laid on one's knee, stomach uppermost. The thumbs are applied to the bottom part of the rabbit's stomach and pushed inwards, being slid down the rabbit's body towards its tail at the same time; the urine is thus expelled. The thumbing should be repeated several times until no more urine appears. If this operation is not carried out, the meat may well be tainted, thus spoiling it. Thumbing is almost invariably carried out in the field, but the next operation, although arguably best carried out in the field too, is very often done at home.

It is necessary to remove the rabbit's intestines before the rabbit can be used for cooking. The operation, referred to as gutting, paunching or dressing out, is simplicity itself and, after a few tries, you will be able to do it with your eyes closed and still finish with a clean product.

To carry out this operation correctly and

relatively easily, you will need a good quality, very sharp knife. If your knife is blunt, the end product will look a mess and you will stand a good chance of cutting yourself. It is a fact that more people receive accidental cuts from blunt knives than they do from sharp ones.

Lay the rabbit on the ground or on a suitable working surface. Gently cut the fur at the bottom of the rib cage and then pull it away from the flesh with your fingers. Next, holding your thumb about three or four millimetres (one tenth of an inch) from the tip of your knife blade, insert the point of the knife into the rabbit (with the cutting edge uppermost) just below the rib cage. The position of your thumb will prevent the point from puncturing the guts; if the intestines are punctured, you will be in for a very messy and smelly job, and the meat may well be tainted. The incision should be just big enough for you to put a couple of fingers in. Now pull the skin open; this will rip quite easily, revealing the rabbit's guts. Splitting like this, instead of cutting with the knife blade, will lessen the risk of rupturing the guts or bladder. Personally, I prefer to use the knife to cut open the skin, thereby giving a much neater appearance – important if the rabbit is to be sold to a game dealer! If you prefer to use the knife, cut very carefully with the cutting edge of the blade uppermost.

Holding the flaps of skin, shake the rabbit with its stomach down towards the ground. This should make all of the guts flop out, but if they do not, insert your fingers behind them and pull them out. If doing this in the field, many ferreters leave the job at this stage (myself included). Some prefer to also remove

Gutting a rabbit. Cut the fur.

Pull open the fur to reveal the skin.

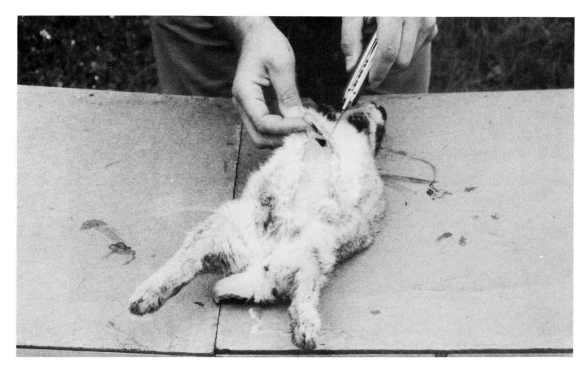

Make an incision. Note that the cutting edge of the blade should be uppermost.

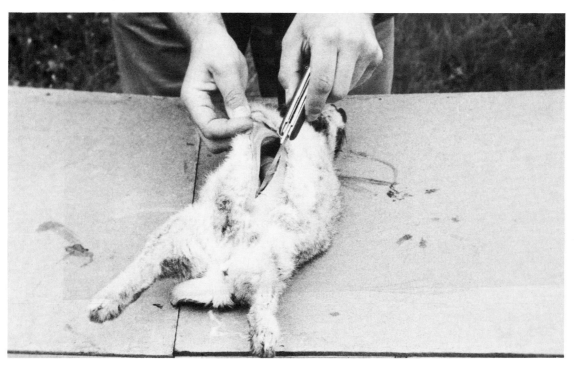

A neater finish is achieved by cutting the skin.

Open the abdomen to expose the rabbit's intestines.

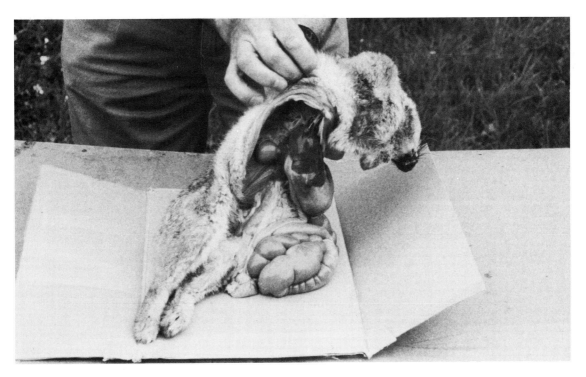

Empty out the intestines.

Clean out the abdomen.

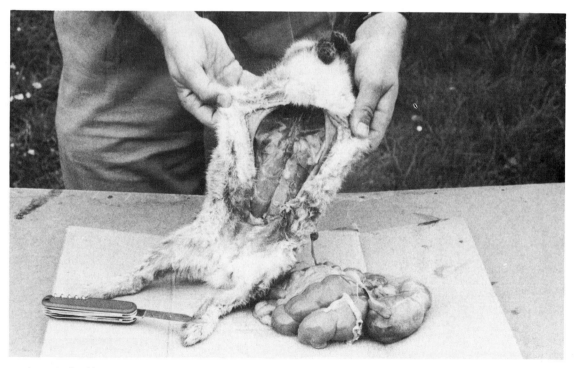

A 'paunched' rabbit.

Skinning a rabbit. Pull the fur away from the animal's body.

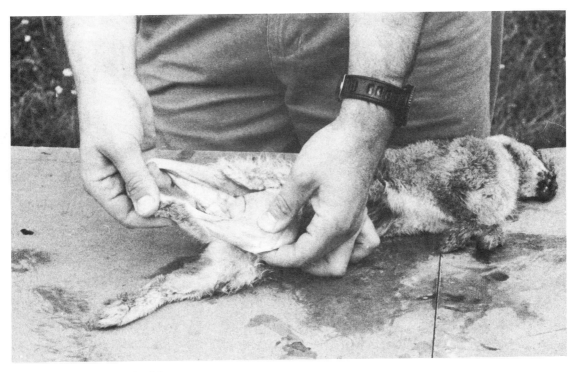

Remove the fur from the hind legs.

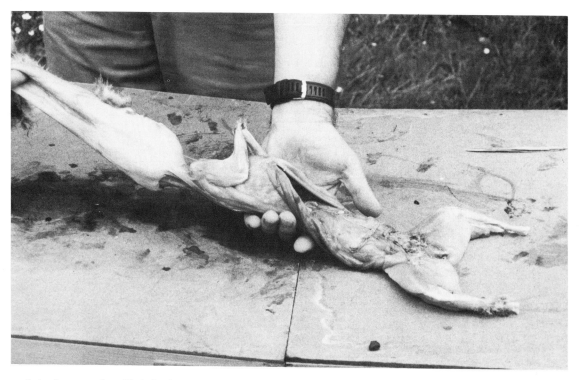

Pull the fur up to the rabbit's head.

Ready for the pot!

the lungs and heart. To do this, cut the diaphragm (the piece of skin across the bottom of the rib cage) and push your fingers up into the chest cavity, pulling out the organs to be found there.

It is worthwhile inspecting the guts for signs of disease. If the liver is covered with small white patches, this is usually a sign of liver fluke. Look for any other signs of infection and check the liver for the gall-bladder. This is a small organ, dark green in colour, and should be carefully trimmed out and thrown away. Its contents are bitter and will spoil the meat if punctured. If there are any obvious signs of disease, the rabbit is best not used for the table.

The rabbit's organs, such as the liver, heart, lungs and kidneys, can be fed to the ferrets. I use these for providing my ferrets with a midday snack during a long hunting foray. I do not believe in waste.

Skinning

The next stage in preparing the rabbit for the table, is skinning. Again, this is a fairly simple operation, and one that gets easier every time it is carried out.

Once the rabbit has been completely gutted, gently ease the skin from the body around the incision that you made to gut the rabbit. This is far easier in recently killed rabbits. Using your fingers, carry on this job until the skin has been separated from the body all the way around the rabbit's torso, so that the hands can be passed around the body under the fur.

Continue this action until the skin has been separated from the back legs; pull the skin all the way off. This usually leaves the fur on from about the knee downwards. Bend the rear legs sharply against the joint, causing the leg to snap and pull off any fur remaining. Cut off the tail and clean out the anus.

Pull the skin towards the front of the rabbit's body, treating the front legs in exactly the same way as the rear legs. Do not continue to attempt to pull skin off at the neck, (over the head) as this is unnecessary. Simply cut the rabbit's head off. This can be separated from the skin and fed to the ferrets.

You are now left with a rabbit ready for the pot, the whole idea of ferreting. Everyone has different tastes but, to me at least, rabbit makes excellent eating. I thought long and hard about the recipes that I would include in this book and decided to simply list a few recipes that I have tried, tested and thoroughly enjoyed. These are all old family recipes, some over half a century old, and I hope that you will enjoy them as much as I have.

It is also possible to turn rabbit into more exotic dishes such as curries or stir-fries, and the recipes for these are to be found in most good cookery books.

Rabbit Recipes

Rabbit Stew

Ingredients
1 rabbit
75g (3oz) fat bacon
1 onion
25g (1oz) flour
600ml (1 pint) water (approx)
salt and pepper
bouquet garni

Method
Joint the rabbit. Cut the bacon into squares and fry for a few minutes and place in casserole. Fry the rabbit in the bacon fat and transfer it to the casserole. Slice the onion, fry to a light brown and transfer to casserole. Add the flour to the remaining fat and fry until brown. Add the water gradually, stir and bring to boiling point to make a smooth sauce. Add salt and pepper, bouquet garni and pour over the rabbit. Cook in the oven for 4 hours at 110C/225F (Gas Mark ¼). Remove bouquet garni before serving.

Rabbit Pie

Ingredients
1 large rabbit
225g (½lb) ham, bacon or pickled pork
5ml (1 teaspoon) chopped parsley
grated lemon rind to flavour
salt and pepper
225g (½lb) rough puff pastry

Method
Cut the rabbit into joints and the ham into slices, and arrange them in alternate layers, with salt, pepper, parsley and lemon rind, in a dish. Add 75ml (5 tablespoons) of water and cover with rough puff pastry. Make a hole in the centre. Cover lightly with grease-proof paper, either at the commencement or preferably after one hour's cooking. Bake for 2 hours at 180°C/350°F (Gas Mark 4). When cooked, pour 150ml (¼ pint) of good seasoned stock into the pie. If the pie is to be served cold, a little gelatine may be dissolved into the stock.

Rabbit and Sage Fricassee

Ingredients
4 large rabbit joints
40g (1½oz) butter
1 onion finely chopped
300ml (½ pint) dry white wine
250ml (8fl oz) chicken stock
8ml (1½ teaspoons) dried sage
15ml (1 tablespoon) chopped parsley
salt and black pepper to taste
8ml (½ tablespoon) plain flour
8ml (½ tablespoon) butter
45ml (3 tablespoons) single cream

Method
Melt the butter in a large pan and fry the chopped onion gently for 4 minutes. Add the rabbit joints and brown. Add the white wine, stock, sage and parsley. Season to taste. Bring to the boil, cover and simmer for 30 minutes or until the rabbit is tender. Remove the joints from the pan and, while creaming the flour and butter to a smooth paste, boil the juices in the pan for 3 minutes. Beat the flour and butter into these juices, a small knob at a time, until the sauce is slightly thickened and smooth. Beat the cream and egg yolk together, and stir it into the sauce. Heat the sauce through but do not allow it to boil. Return the rabbit joints to the pan, heat through and transfer to a warm serving dish. Garnish with croutons.

Roast Rabbit

Ingredients
1 rabbit
75ml (4 tablespoons) breadcrumbs
30ml (2 tablespoons) chopped suet
30ml (2 tablespoons) chopped ham
5ml (1 teaspoon) mixed herbs
5ml (1 teaspoon) chopped parsley
grated rind of half a lemon
pepper and salt
1 egg
50g (2oz) dripping or fat bacon

Method
Wipe the rabbit and season inside with a little salt and pepper. Prepare the stuffing with the above ingredients and put inside the rabbit. Skewer the head back and the legs on each side. Cover the rabbit with dripping or fat bacon, place in a well-greased baking tin and cook at 220C/425F (Gas Mark 7) for 1¼ hours, or until tender. Serve with braised parsnip, carrots and baked potatoes.

Keepers' Casserole

Ingredients
4 Rabbit Legs
100g (4oz) smoked streaky bacon
50g (2oz) butter
30ml (2 tablespoons) vegetable oil
1 medium onion – peeled and chopped
1 stick celery chopped
1 medium carrot – peeled and sliced thinly
1 clove garlic peeled and crushed
150ml (¼ pint) dry white wine
60ml (2fl oz) red wine
60ml (2fl oz) red wine vinegar
5ml (1 teaspoon) dried rosemary
5 juniper berries
2 bay leaves
salt and black pepper to taste

Method
Cut each rabbit leg in half and make half-inch-deep cuts in the flesh. Cut the bacon into small pieces and insert into the cuts in the rabbit flesh. Melt the butter and oil in a large flame proof casserole, add the rabbit pieces and fry over a moderate heat until brown. Remove from the pan and set aside. Add the onion, celery, carrot and garlic and fry over a gentle heat, stirring frequently until softened and browned. Return the rabbit pieces to the casserole, add the remaining ingredients and season to taste. Bring to the boil slowly, cover and cook in a preheated oven 160°C/325°F (Gas Mark 3) until the rabbit is tender – approximately 2 hours.

Bon appetit!

Glossary

Albino A white (although often appears yellowish) ferret, with seemingly pink eyes – the eyes are actually colourless, but the blood vessels behind them give them a pink appearance.

Bolters The loose working ferrets employed to make rabbits (or rats) bolt from their underground home. The rabbits that bolt are also referred to by the same name.

Burrow A series of underground tunnels, all interconnected, in which wild rabbits live. Sometimes referred to as a 'bury'.

Business A group of ferrets – the term is very rarely used these days.

Chad The round-bladed spade used for digging out dead rabbits and errant ferrets. It is also known as a graft.

Collar A collar is placed around the neck of the liner ferret and a line attached to it. Pet ferrets are often put on to a collar and lead and taken for walks.

Cub The hutch-like cage that many ferrets are kept in.

Court A cage rather like an aviary, in which ferrets are kept.

Dig The task of digging to and removing rabbits or ferrets from underground.

Draw-string The string or cord which is threaded through the top of a purse net. It is this draw-string which operates the purse net.

Dressing out The removal of a rabbit's internal organs and intestines. Sometimes called 'paunching'.

Electronic detector A device for tracking ferrets (and terriers) while they are working underground. The device consists of a collar mounted transmitter and a hand-held receiver. Both are pre-tuned. A modern detector can be used to a depth of almost eight feet.

Ferret The domesticated European polecat (*Mustella putorius*). The term is often used to describe only the albino version of this species.

Ferret detector *See* Electronic detector.

Filling in The task of returning an area of dug earth (e.g. after a 'dig') to its original condition. This is a thankless and onerous task, but one which must always be carried out after any digging.

Fitch The ferret's fur.

Fitchet A term used to describe the offspring of a mating between a polecat and an albino ferret. The term was originally used to describe the young of a wild polecat and a domesticated ferret, but today it is used for the progeny of any mating between a coloured polecat (or ferret) and an albino ferret.

Fleck Small pieces of rabbit fur. Their presence on a ferret's foot during a hunting trip indicates that the ferret has been in physical contact with a rabbit, perhaps even killing it.

Foot rot A disease caused by mites and resulting in the feet of the afflicted ferret quite literally rotting; once thought to be caused solely by the ferrets being kept in dirty and wet conditions.

Form Grassy hollows, where rabbits often sit during the daytime.

Free workers Ferrets which are allowed to hunt through the burrow without any line attached (although sometimes wearing an elecronic transmitter, to enable the ferreter to track it). Usually, but not always, jill (female) ferrets.

Game carrier A device for carrying game (in this case rabbits), usually over one's shoulder, instead of hocking the rabbits.

Gestation Pregnancy. In ferrets, this is between forty and forty-four days.

Graft *See* 'Chad'.

Greyhound ferret A tiny, agile ferret. Sometimes referred to as a 'whippet ferret'.

Gun When written with a capital 'G', this refers to the person actually using a shotgun.

Heat A term often used to describe oestrus.

Heatstroke The effect of too much heat on a ferret. If this condition is not treated, it can be fatal. Sometimes referred to as 'the sweats'.

Hob A male ferret or polecat.

Hobble A castrated hob.

Hocking The method of passing a dead rabbit's rear leg through an incision made in the other rear leg (between the leg bone and the tendon), in order that the rabbits may be carried easier. Sometimes referred to as 'legging'.

Hybrid A cross-bred ferret. The term can either mean the offspring of a wild polecat and a domesticated ferret or the progeny of the mating of a closely bred animal with a completely unrelated one.

Hybrid vigour The increased vigour and resistance to disease often found in the offspring of completely unrelated ferrets.

In-breeding The practice of breeding very closely related ferrets together.

Jill A female ferret or polecat.

Kit or Kitten A young ferret. Usually used to describe a ferret of twelve weeks of age or less (the same terms are also used to describe young rabbits).

Lay-up Where a ferret has killed one or more rabbits and then settled down (usually to sleep) next to the body.

Legging *See* Hocking

Line breeding A moderate form of in-breeding.

Liner A large solitary hob, attached to the end of a line (hence his name) and used to find dead rabbits underground. Recently, the liner has been made almost redundant with the introduction of new technology, in the shape of the electronic ferret detector.

Litter The young ferrets produced at one birth.

Long net A net used for catching bolting rabbits that escaped the purse nets.

Mask The markings on the face of a polecat (or polecat ferret). This mask is usually darker in the summer than in the winter.

Musk The foul-smelling scent produced by the anal glands of ferrets and polecats.

Muzzle A device for preventing the ferret from biting (either humans or his natural quarry). Made from leather, string or metal; they must never be used on ferrets while they are working.

Myxomatosis A deadly viral disease amongst rabbits. Thought to have been deliberately introduced to this country from France, to control the numbers of wild rabbits here.

Oestrus The state in which a jill will accept a mating (*See also* Heat).

Ovulation The release of eggs into the womb to be fertilised by the hob's sperm.

Parasites Animals which live on or in other animals (hosts) and are detrimental to the host. Includes worms, fleas, mites, lice and ticks.

Paunching *See* Dressing out.

Peeing The squeezing out of the urine of a dead rabbit with the thumbs. Often referred to as 'thumbing'. This is a necessary operation to prevent the rabbit's flesh from becoming tainted (and therefore inedible) with the urine.

Photoperiodism The dependence on the daytime/night-time ratio of various biological functions, particularly the commencement of oestrus.

Polecat The common name of the animal *Mustella putorius*. Strictly, this name should only be used to describe the wild polecat, but today it is also commonly used to describe any domesticated ferret with polecat-type markings.

Poley A domesticated ferret with the typical wild polecat markings.

Priest A small club, often with one end weighted with lead, used for killing netted rabbits.

Probe A blunted iron rod with a bulge in it. Used to locate underground passages, especially during a dig to a liner.

Purse net A nylon or hemp net with a draw-string threaded through the outer parts, resembling the old-fashioned draw-string purse. When properly set up, a bolting rabbit entering the net will cause it to purse, thus trapping the rabbit.

Sandy A coloured ferret with colouring between an albino and a polecat.

Scours Diarrhoea.

Set A small bury.

Skulk When a ferret refuses to leave the mouth of a tunnel into the open air, it is said to be 'skulking'.

Sops Bread and milk, sometimes (though often wrongly) fed to ferrets.

Stop A dead-ended tunnel in a bury, originally built to be the nursery for a litter of rabbit kittens.

Sweats *See* Heatstroke.

Swivel A device attached to a ferret's collar, on to which is fastened the line.

Thumbing *See* Peeing.

Warren A very large bury.

Bibliography

Bateman, J. A., *Animal Traps and Trapping* (David and Charles, 1971)

Bouchner, Miroslav, *Animal Tracks and Traces* (Octopus, 1982)

Burton, John and Pearson, Bruce, *Rare Mammals of the World* (Collins, 1987)

Clutton-Brock, Juliet, *A Natural History of Domesticated Animals* (Cambridge University Press and the British Museum (Natural History), 1987)

Cooper, J.E., Hutchinson, M.F., Jackson, O.F. and Maurice, R.J. (eds.), *Manual of Exotic Pets* (The British Small Animal Veterinary Association, 1985)

Cooper, Margaret, LLB, *An Introduction to Animal Law* (The Academic Press, 1977)

Corbet, G.B. and Hill, J.E., *A World List of Mammalian Species* (The British Museum (Natural History), 1980)

Everitt, N., *Ferrets – Their Management in Health and Disease* (N. Everitt, 1897)

Ewer, R.F., *The Carnivores* (Weidenfeld and Nicholson, 1973)

Gouldsbury, Pat (ed.), *Predatory Mammals in Britain* (The National Council for Nature, 1967)

Grzimek, B., *Grzimek's Animal Life Encyclopedia* (Vols 10, 11 and 12) (Van Nostrad Reinhold, 1972)

Honacki, J.H. and Kinman, K.E., *Mammal Species of the World* (Allen Press, 1982)

Lawrence, M.J. and Brown, R.W., *Mammals of Britain* (Blandford Press, 1967)

Lever, Christopher, *The Naturalised Animals of the British Isles* (Hutchinson and Co., 1977)

Lockley, R.M., *The Private Life of the Rabbit* (Andre Deutsch, 1965)

MacDonald, Dr David, *The Encyclopedia of Mammals* (Vol 1) (Guild, 1985)

Marchington, John, *Pugs and Drummers* (Faber and Faber, 1978)

Mason, I.L. (ed.), *The Evolution of Domesticated Animals* (Longman, 1984)

Mathews, L. Harrison, *The Life of Mammals* (Weidenfeld and Nicholson, 1971)
  British Mammals (Collins, 1968)

Morris, Desmond, *The Mammals* (Hodder and Stoughton, 1965)

Pardiso, Nowak, *Walker's Mammals of the World* (Johns Hopkins University Press, 1983)

Parkes, Charlie and Thornley, John, *Fair Game* (Pelham Books, 1987)

Pinniger, R.S. (ed.), *Jones' Animal Nursing* (Pergamon Press, 1972)

Plummer, Brian, *Modern Ferreting* (The Boydell Press, 1977)
  Tales of a Rat Hunting Man (The Boydell Press, 1978)

Porter, Val and Brown, Nicholas, *The Complete Book of Ferrets* (Pelham Books, 1985)

Roberts, Mervin F., *All About Ferrets,* (TFH, 1977)

Samuel, E. and Ivester Lloyd, J., *Rabbiting and Ferreting* (The British Field Sports Society, 1966)

Southern, H.M., *The Handbook of British Mammals* (The Mammal Society)

Taylor, Fred J., *The Shooting Times Guide to Ferreting* (Buchan and Enright, 1983)

The Game Conservancy, *Rabbit Control* (MAFF and the Game Conservancy, 1980)

Twigg, Graham, *The Brown Rat,* (David and Charles, 1975)

Turner, Gerry D. (ed.), *Handbook of Shooting* (Pelham Books with the British Association for Shooting and Conservation, 1983)

Ucko, P.J., *The Domestication and Exploitation of Plants and Animals* (Duckworth, 1971)

Universities Federation for Animal Welfare, *The UFAW Handbook on the Care and Management of Laboratory Animals* (Churchill Livingstone, 1976)

Watson, A.E.T., *The Rabbit* (Ashford Press, 1986)

Welstead, Graham, *The Ferret and Ferreting Guide* (David and Charles, 1981)

West, Geoffrey (ed.), *Black's Veterinary Dictionary* (A. and C. Black, 1988)

Whitaker, Peter, *Ferrets and Ferreting* (Pugs and Drummers, 1978)

Winstead, Wendy, *Ferrets* (TFH, 1982)

Useful Addresses and Magazines

Organisations

When writing to any of the following, please enclose a self-addressed, stamped envelope, as all voluntary organisations depend upon income from membership subscriptions. Funds are, therefore, at a premium. As some of the groups have no paid staff, please bear in mind that honorary officers will, from time to time, change.

The Association of British Wild Animal Keepers
c/o Penscynor Wildlife Park
Cilfrew
Neath
West Glamorgan
Tel. (0639) 2189

This Association was founded in 1974 to 'further a common interest in wild animals', the emphasis being placed upon the husbandry of wild animals in captivity. As such, ABWAK is not specifically interested in ferreting, but members of the Association possess a wealth of knowledge and information on many animals, including the *mustelidae*. The Association's journal, *Ratel,* is a superb publication and contains many articles that will be of interest to owners/breeders of ferrets. *Ratel* is only available to members of ABWAK.

The British Association for Shooting and Conservation
Marford Mill
Rossett
Wrexham
Clwyd LL12 0HL
Tel. (0244) 570881

Formerly known as the Wildfowlers' Association of Great Britain and Ireland (WAGBI), membership of this association is highly recommended as, apart from many intangible benefits (such as protection of the sport), membership provides third party liability cover for all members whilst engaged in shooting or conservation activities.

The British Field Sports Society
59 Kennington Road
London SE1 7PZ
Tel. (01) 928 4742

Probably the only society that defends all country sports, membership is advisable, if only to register support for country sports.

The Fell and Moorland Working Terrier Club
c/o I. D. Rainbow, Esq.
79 Groveley Lane
West Heath
Birmingham B31 4QQ
Tel. (021) 475 4966

The Field and Country Sports Society of Ireland
c/o M. C. A. Jackson, Esq.
Ferndale
Kilpedder
Greystones
Co. Wicklow
Tel. (08494) 874317

The Game Conservancy
Fordingbridge
Hants SP6 1EF
Tel. (0425) 52381

The Kennel Club
1 Clarges Street
London W1
Tel. (01) 493 6651

The National Farmers' Union
Agriculture House
Knightsbridge
London SW1
Tel. (01) 235 5077

The National Ferret Welfare Society
c/o Mrs Kim Lathaen
Meadow View
Pheasant's Hill
Hambleden
Henley-on-Thames RG9 6SN
Tel. (0491) 571512

Everyone with an interest in ferrets and/or
ferreting should be a member of this society.
Until such time as everyone is, the humble
ferret will never be seen and respected for
what she really is – a marvellous, brave and
friendly creature.

The National Game Dealers' Association
c/o J. E. Fuller, Esq.
1 Belgrove
Tunbridge Wells
Kent TN1 1YW
Tel. (0892) 44046

The National Lurcher Racing Club
c/o A. McCurry, Esq.
21 Old Church Road
Bell Green
Coventry CV6 7BZ
Tel. (0203) 664087

The Students' Country Sports Campaign
Marford Mill
Rossett
Wrexham
Clwyd LL12 0HL
Tel. (0244) 570881

**The Universities Federation for Animal
Welfare (UFAW)**
8 Hamilton Close
South Mimms
Potter's Bar
Middlesex EN6 3QD
Tel. (0707) 58202

Magazines

The following magazines all carry regular or
occasional articles of interest to ferret keepers.

Country Life
Available from newsagents
Editorial address: King Reach Tower,
Stamford Street, London SE1 9LS
Tel. (01) 261 5000

Countrysport
A monthly magazine which is available from
newsagents.
Editorial address: 47 Church Street, Barnsley,
South Yorkshire S70 2AS
Tel. (0226) 203203

The Field
Published monthly, this magazine is available
from all good newsagents.
Editorial Address: Mail Newspapers, plc.,
Carmelite House, London EC4Y 0JA
Tel. (01) 353 6000

Insight
A quarterly magazine, available from
newsagents.
Editorial address: 45 Eastgate, Bourne,
Lincolnshire PE10 9JT
Tel. (0778) 421532

Ratel
The Journal of the Association of British Wild
Animal Keepers. Published monthly, it is only
available to members. Full membership details
may be obtained from Mrs Kate Partridge, 2a
Northcote Road, Clifton, Bristol BS8 3HB
Tel. (0272) 736480

USEFUL ADDRESSES AND MAGAZINES

Shooting and Conservation

The quarterly magazine of the British Association for Shooting and Conservation (BASC). It is only available to members. Membership details may be obtained from the Membership Department, BASC Headquarters, Marford Mill, Rossett, Wrexham, Clwyd LL12 0HL.
Tel. (0244) 570881

Shooting Life

Published monthly, this magazine is available from newsagents.
Editorial address: Romsey Publishing Limited, 2 The Courtyard, Denmark Street, Wokingham, Berkshire RG11 21W
Tel. (0734) 771677

Shooting News

Available from newsagents, this magazine is published weekly.
Editorial address: Unit 2, Plymouth Road Industrial Estate, Tavistock, Devon PL19 9QN
Tel. (0822) 616460

Shooting Times

One of the oldest country sports magazines, the magazine is published weekly and is available from all good newsagents. It is the official weekly journal of the British Association of Shooting and Conservation.
Editorial address: 10 Sheet Street, Windsor, Berkshire SL4 1BG
Tel. (0753) 856061

Sporting Gun

A monthly magazine, available from newsagents.
Editorial address: EMAP Publications, Bretton, Peterborough PE3 8DZ
Tel. (0733) 264666

Index

INDEX